HAN FEI TZU

W9-CCY-678

Prepared for the Columbia College Program of
Translations from the Oriental Classics
WM. THEODORE DE BARY, *Editor*

HAN FEI TZU

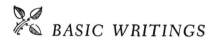 *BASIC WRITINGS*

Translated by BURTON WATSON

New York

COLUMBIA UNIVERSITY PRESS

Preparation of this work was done under a grant from the Carnegie Corporation of New York to the Committee on Oriental Studies for the production of texts to be used in undergraduate education. That Corporation is not, however, the author, owner, publisher, or proprietor of this publication, and is not to be understood as approving by virtue of its grant any of the statements made or views expressed.

UNESCO COLLECTION OF REPRESENTATIVE WORKS—CHINESE SERIES
This work has been accepted in the Chinese Translation Series of the United Nations Educational, Scientific, and Cultural Organization (UNESCO).

ISBN 0-231-08609-1
Library of Congress Catalog Card Number: 64-13734
Printed in the United States of America
p 20 19

FOREWORD

Han Fei Tzu: Basic Writings is one of a group of publications, the Translations from the Oriental Classics, through which the Committee on Oriental Studies has sought to transmit to Western readers representative works of the Oriental traditions in thought and literature. In its volumes of source readings forming the "Introduction to Oriental Civilizations," the Committee has provided a broad selection of excerpts from influential thinkers in India, China, and Japan, discussing the great problems of their times. Excerpts from Han Fei Tzu are thus included in *Sources of Chinese Tradition*. Several of the great philosophers of classical China, however, deserve a fuller reading and analysis than such a survey allows, and there has been a need for more complete translations of them. To say this is not to deprecate the excellent work already done by pioneer scholars in opening these writers up to the West. Often, however, their translations have not been kept in print or available at prices most readers could afford. To give them much wider circulation in the home and classroom than heretofore is the aim of this series.

We are indebted to Professor Watson that he has been willing to devote his considerable talents and learning to meet this need for accurate translations of basic works. No doubt it would have been personally more gratifying to the researcher's instinct in him, and in the professional fraternity, had he turned to some untouched subject, no matter how obscure and out-of-the-way. That he has returned to several of the old masters is a credit both to them and to him. Great figures like Han Fei Tzu, Mo Tzu, Hsün Tzu, and Chuang Tzu, merit rediscovery and reexamination by each generation. How much more is this true when, in comparison to Confucius and Lao Tzu, they have been known until now by so few!

WM. THEODORE DE BARY

CONTENTS

FOREWORD, *by Wm. Theodore de Bary*   v

PREFACE   ix

OUTLINE OF EARLY CHINESE HISTORY   xii

INTRODUCTION   1

THE WAY OF THE RULER   16

ON HAVING STANDARDS   21

THE TWO HANDLES   30

WIELDING POWER   35

THE EIGHT VILLAINIES   43

THE TEN FAULTS   49

THE DIFFICULTIES OF PERSUASION   73

MR. HO   80

PRECAUTIONS WITHIN THE PALACE   84

FACING SOUTH   90

THE FIVE VERMIN   96

EMINENCE IN LEARNING   118

INDEX   130

PREFACE

Surely one of the most startling and spectacular archeological finds of the present century was the huge cache of life-size terra-cotta figures of Ch'in-period warriors and officials that was discovered near the tomb of the first Ch'in ruler in China in 1974. Though restorers had to spend considerable time piecing together the crumbled images, when they revealed their finds to the public, it was as though the Ch'in dynasty, which ruled China from 221 to 207 B.C., had suddenly come to life again, its men and horses miraculously rising up out of the ground before the astonished eyes of the world.

Though the philosopher Han Fei Tzu did not live to see the Ch'in dynasty, his writings were known to and admired by its founder, the First Emperor; and historical records depict his successor, the Second Emperor, as quoting from the "Five Vermin" chapter, one of the chapters translated in the selection that follows. Indeed, Han Fei Tzu's name has become inextricably linked with that of the Ch'in dynasty, since the First Emperor openly espoused the principles of the Legalist school of philosophy, of which Han Fei Tzu was a leading proponent. These same Legalist doctrines have also been blamed for the rapidity with which the Ch'in dynasty fell from power, though one might argue that it was not so much the doctrines themselves as the severity and ineptness with which the Ch'in rulers applied them that brought on catastrophe. Han Fei Tzu, for example, had urged rulers to make haste in designating their heirs and successors—a piece of advice that the First Emperor ignored, with the most dire consequences.

The Ch'in dynasty, toppled by internal revolt, its vast palaces burned to the ground, went out of existence in 207 B.C.; the army of terra-cotta figures was hidden underground and totally forgotten until its accidental discovery in 1974. The writings of Han Fei Tzu, on the other hand, have never ceased to be a part of the Chinese literary heritage, challenging readers with their trenchant discourses on the nature and use of political power, inspiring assent or violent aversion but seldom mere indifference. In the past they were known mainly to countries within the Chinese cultural sphere; now, thanks to translations into other languages, they have become a part of world thought. I am gratified that these selected translations of mine, done some thirty years ago, continue to be made available to the English-reading public in this new format.

BURTON WATSON

OUTLINE OF EARLY CHINESE HISTORY

(Dates and entries before 841 B.C. are traditional)

B.C.	Dynasty	
2852		Fu Hsi, inventor of writing, fishing, trapping.
2737	Culture Heroes	Shen Nung, inventor of agriculture, commerce.
2697		Yellow Emperor.
2357	Sage Kings	Yao.
2255		Shun.
2205		Yü, virtuous founder of dynasty.
1818	Hsia Dynasty	Chieh, degenerate terminator of dynasty.
1766	Shang or Yin Dynasty	King T'ang, virtuous founder of dynasty.
[c. 1300]		[Beginning of archeological evidence.]
1154		Chou, degenerate terminator of dynasty.

	Three Dynasties	1122	King Wen, virtuous founder of dynasty.
		1115	King Wu, virtuous founder of dynasty.
Chou Dynasty	Western Chou		King Ch'eng, virtuous founder of dynasty.
			(Duke of Chou, regent to King Ch'eng)
		878	King Li.
		781	King Yu.
		771	
		722	Spring and Autumn period (722–481).
	Eastern Chou	551	Period of the "hundred philosophers" (551–c. 233): Confucius, Mo Tzu, Lao Tzu (?), Mencius, Chuang Tzu, Hui Shih, Shang Yang, Kung-sun Lung, Hsün Tzu, Han Fei Tzu.
		403	Warring States period (403–221).
		4th to 3d cent.	Extensive wall-building and waterworks by Ch'in and other states.
		249	Lü Pu-wei, prime minister of Ch'in.
Ch'in Dynasty (221–207 B.C.)		221	The First Emperor; Li Ssu, prime minister.
		214	The Great Wall completed.

INTRODUCTION

As in the case of most early Chinese philosophers, little is known of the life of Han Fei Tzu, or Master Han Fei. We are fortunate, however, in the few facts we have, for they supply us with a motive and setting for his writings, and an account of his death which, whatever its reliability as history, adds a fine touch of dramatic irony.

So far as we know, Han Fei was the only nobleman among the important early Chinese philosophers. Confucius, Mo Tzu, Mencius, Chuang Tzu, Hsün Tzu seem to have been men of the lower gentry, descendants perhaps of aristocratic families that had sunk into poverty and no longer occupied a position of any real power in the feudal hierarchy of the day. Hence, as we see from their lives, though they manifested the customary loyalty and respect toward the ruler of their native state, they did not hesitate to travel about visiting other rulers, settle in other states, or withdraw from the world entirely. The very humbleness of their birth allowed them a freedom of thought and movement that was denied to the noblemen above them in the social scale, as it was to the peasants beneath them.

Han Fei, by contrast, was a prince of the royal family of the state of Han. This accident of birth saddled him with responsibilities that his fellow philosophers did not share and bound his fate inexorably to that of his native state; in the end, it brought about his death.

The small state of Han was situated in central China in the region south and east of the Chou capital at Loyang. Its ruling family had formerly been high ministers in the state of Chin, and had gradually usurped power until, with two other ministerial families, they divided up the territory of Chin and created the three new states of Han, Wei, and Chao, a move which finally received official recognition from the Chou ruler in 403 B.C. The rulers of Han, originally titled marquises, in time assumed the title of king. But their domain was small and situated in a mountainous and unproductive region, and they were constantly threatened by predatory neighbors, particularly the powerful state of Ch'in directly to the west.

The date of Han Fei's birth is unknown, though scholars place it tentatively around 280 B.C. His biography in the *Shih chi*, or *Records of the Historian* (ch. 63), written some hundred years after his death by the historian Ssu-ma Ch'ien, states that he studied under the eminent Confucian philosopher Hsün Tzu. This was probably during the period when Hsün Tzu was serving as magistrate of Lan-ling, a region in southern Shantung, that is, around 250 B.C. One of Han Fei's fellow students was Li Ssu (d. 208 B.C.), the man who was destined to become prime minister and chief aid to the First Emperor of the Ch'in dynasty and to play a sinister role in Han Fei's life.

Fate not only inflicted on Han Fei the burden of noble birth in a state whose fortunes were dim and precarious, but added an extra fillip. He stuttered badly—in an age when eloquence was a potent political weapon and the glibbest statesmen were usually the most successful. His biography records that, distressed by the dangerous condition of his native state, he repeatedly submitted letters of remonstrance to its ruler, presumably King Huan-hui (r. 272–239 B.C.), or his successor King An (r. 238–230 B.C.). But the king was unwilling to heed his advice and Han Fei, prevented by his disability from expounding his ideas aloud, took the only course left open: he wrote a book. His biography mentions by name several of the essays included in it, among them "The Five Vermin" and "The Difficulties of Persuasion," both translated here.

In time Han Fei's writings came into the hands of the king of Ch'in, the youthful ruler who had ascended the throne of Ch'in in 246 B.C. and was soon to conquer and rule all China under the title of First Emperor of the Ch'in dynasty. He expressed great admiration for them to his minister Li Ssu, who revealed the identity of their author. The king's admiration, however, did not deter him from launching a fierce attack on Han Fei's native state in 234 B.C. The ruler of Han, King An, who had earlier refused to heed Han Fei's advice, at the eleventh hour decided to dispatch the philosopher as his envoy to Ch'in in hopes of saving his state from destruction. Han Fei journeyed to the Ch'in court and was received with delight by the king. But before he could gain the king's full confidence, his former fellow student, Li Ssu, intervened, warning the king that, since Han Fei was a member of the royal family of Han, his loyalties would always be on the side of Han and against Ch'in. Whether Li Ssu acted out of sincere concern for the state or mere personal jealousy, we shall never know; in any event, he succeeded in persuading the Ch'in ruler to hand the philosopher over to the law officials for investigation. Before the king of Ch'in might have time to regret this decision (as he later did), Li Ssu sent poison to the prison where Han Fei was confined, near the summer palace at Sweet Springs. Han Fei, unable to communicate with the ruler and defend himself against the charge of duplicity, drank the poison. The year was 233 B.C., and he was probably in his forties or early fifties.

Han Fei Tzu is a representative of the school of philosophy known as *Fa-chia*, the Legalist or Realist school. He is not the inventor of Legalism, but its perfecter, having left us the final and most readable exposition of its theories. Some of the ideas and policies of Legalism are said to date as early as the seventh century, when the statesman Kuan Chung (d. 645 B.C.) brought wealth and power to the state of Ch'i by applying them, though reliable evidence is scanty. The *Kuan Tzu*, a work supposed to embody the teachings of Kuan Chung, contains sections expounding Legalist ideas, but these almost certainly date from late Chou times. Another typically Legalist work, the *Shang-chün shu*, or *Book of Lord Shang*, is attributed to the statesman Wei Yang or Kung-sun Yang (d. 338 B.C.), who served as a high minister in the state of Ch'in. With its strong emphasis upon strict control of the people by harsh laws, and the encouragement of agriculture and agressive warfare, it very well may reflect the actual policies of Wei Yang, though it was probably not written until some years after his death. Two other Legalist or semi-Legalist books, both of them now lost, undoubtedly influenced Han Fei Tzu. One was the work of Shen Tao, a Taoist-Legalist thinker about whom little is known; the other was the work of Shen Pu-hai, a Legalist philosopher who served at the court of Han Fei's native state and died there in 337 B.C. From these various works, particularly the *Book of Lord Shang* and the writings of Shen Pu-hai, Han Fei Tzu culled his ideas, combining what seemed to him the best features of each and welding them into a clear and comprehensive whole.

Comprehensive, that is, within the rather circumscribed interests of Legalist philosophy. All Chinese philosophical systems are concerned to some extent with questions of political science, but none so exclusively as Legalism. All the extant writings of the Legalist school deal with a single problem: how to preserve and strengthen the state. Like Machiavelli's famous treatise, to which it has often been compared, Han Fei Tzu's work is a handbook for the prince, with a few chapters thoughtfully added for the guidance of his ministers.

The rulers of China in late Chou times had need for such a handbook. In the earlier days of Chou feudalism the rights and duties of the ruler and his vassals had presumably been fairly clearly defined. During Western Chou times (1027–771 B.C.), the Chou king not only commanded universal allegiance and respect among his vassals, but apparently exercised considerable control over their affairs, intervening in matters of succession or even executing an offending vassal. But after the Chou ruler was forced by barbarian invasion in 771 B.C. to flee from his capital and establish his court at Loyang in the east, his power steadily waned, and the rulers of the feudal states were left increasingly free to ignore the customary duties to the sovereign and to each other if they pleased.

In time, a succession of powerful feudal leaders, known as the Five *Pa*—dictators or hegemons—rose to prominence to fill the political vacuum, imposing their will upon the Chou king and the other feudal lords and restoring a semblance of over-all authority to China. The first of these, Duke Huan of Ch'i (r. 685–643 B.C.), according to later accounts, carried out a series of administrative reforms suggested by his minister Kuan Chung which enriched his state, increased the efficiency of its armies, and gave the ruler more direct control of the population. It is hard to say just how far the details of these accounts are to be trusted. But certainly in a number of states in middle and late Chou times reforms were instituted, the purpose of which was to strengthen the central government, to gain more effective control of land and population, and to replace the old aristocracy with a bureaucracy appointed by the ruler. Though probably of limited scope and effectiveness at first, such reforms became more drastic as the old feudal order decayed, and states that failed to adopt them fell dangerously behind the times. The state of Chin, which was overthrown and dismembered by its ministerial families in 403 B.C., seems to have foundered mainly for this reason.

These administrative reforms, along with technological advances in agriculture and warfare, allowed the large states to annex their feebler neighbors or to push back the frontiers of China and open up new lands for cultivation. The new territories acquired in these ways were not, in most cases, parceled out as fiefs, but were incorporated into the state as prefectures and districts under the control of the central government, a practice that foreshadowed the final abolition of feudalism under the Ch'in dynasty. Changes were taking place in the system of land tenure; in the more advanced states, land could be bought and sold, and peasants could hire themselves out as day laborers. The old ceremonies and obligations that had held together the fabric of feudal society fell into neglect, and the rulers were left without a set of rules to guide them in the administration of their states or the conduct of their foreign affairs. Some of them drew up law codes for the governance of internal affairs, but no one was in a position to draw up or enforce a code of international law, and relations between states were marked by intrigue, deceit, and ruthless pursuit of self-interest.

This was the situation when Legalism made its appearance as a recognizable school of thought. It addressed itself exclusively to the rulers, taking no interest in private individuals or their lives except to the extent that they affected the interests of the ruling class. Unlike Confucianism and Moism, it made no attempt to preserve or restore the customs and moral values of the past; indeed, it professed to have no use for morality whatsoever. Religious beliefs and ceremonies likewise, at least as far as the ruling class was concerned, it regarded as fatuous and distracting, and looked upon the fondness for such ceremonies as the mark of a doomed state. Its only goal was to teach the ruler, in what it regarded as hardheaded and practical terms, how to survive and prosper in the world of the present.

Its techniques were those which we have already noted as actually being carried out in some states: the strengthening of the central government, the establishment of more effective control over land and population through laws and strict penalties, and the replacement of the old aristocracy by a corps of bureaucrats. In particular it emphasized the encouragement of agriculture to provide a steady food supply and of warfare to expand the borders of the state and insure a tough, alert, and well-disciplined population. It called for the suppression of all ideas and ways of life that impeded the realization of these aims. Vagabonds and draft-dodgers, merchants and artisans who deal in nonessential goods, scholars who spread doctrines at variance with Legalist teaching, cavaliers who take the law into their own hands—all were to be unmercifully quashed, and the people to be kept in a state of ignorance and awe.

The ideas outlined above are all to be found in the writings of Han Fei Tzu. He adopted them from the *Book of Lord Shang*, along with that work's concept of *fa*—the elaborate system of laws that are to be drawn up by the ruler, distributed to his officials, and taught and explained by them to the illiterate populace. By such a system of laws, and the inescapable punishments that back it up, all life within the nation was to be ordered, so that nothing would be left to chance, private judgment, or the appeal to privilege.

But the concept of law represents only one aspect of Han Fei Tzu's system, the aspect that is concerned with the ruler's control and administration of the population as a whole. To this he added a second concept borrowed from the writings of Shen Pu-hai, the concept of *shu*—policies, methods, or arts of governing. The officials and the people at large may be guided and kept in line by laws. But the ruler, who is the author of law and outside and above it, must be guided by a different set of principles. These principles constitute his *shu,* the policies and arts which he applies in wielding authority and controlling the men under him.

As the more powerful states of late Chou times grew in size and their governments became more centralized, numerous problems of administration arose that had no precedent for solution in the practices of the earlier feudalism. To break the power of the old aristocracy, the rulers deliberately selected men from the lower ranks of society who would be less encumbered by clan loyalties and more dependent upon the good will of the ruler, and promoted them to administrative posts. But if the ruler was to remain secure in his position, he had to find ways to control his newly created bureaucracy, which constantly expanded as the concerns of government became more complex and far-reaching. Unable any longer to attend to all affairs in person, he had to make certain that the men to whom he delegated power were doing their work efficiently and without deceit. He needed, in other words, a set of rules for management and personnel control, and this was what Han Fei Tzu supplied under the name of *shu*.

From the logicians Han Fei Tzu borrowed the term *hsing-ming*—literally, "forms and names." The members of the School of Names, and the other thinkers of the period who took an interest in problems of semantics, used the term to emphasize the need for an exact correspondence between the name of a thing and its actual form or reality. Han Fei Tzu, when he took over the term, ignored its more abstract philosophical connotations and gave it a specifically political interpretation. By "names" he meant the name of the office a man held, the list of duties he was expected to perform, or the proposals he made; by "forms" he meant the actual performance of the man in office; and he insisted that only when these two coincided exactly could the man be regarded as doing his job properly. He therefore urged the ruler to keep constant check upon the correspondence between names and forms. If they tallied, the man was to be rewarded and promoted; if they failed to tally—whether the man had done less than his office called for or more—he was to be summarily punished.

From Taoism Han Fei Tzu borrowed a second set of ideas which goes to make up the concept of *shu*. Taoist philosophy, with its doctrine of quietism and its transcendence of worldly concerns and values, may seem an odd place to go in search of ideas on how to run a government. But Taoist and Legalist thought seem to have been curiously interrelated from early times, though the paucity of sources makes it impossible to say exactly why or how.

Nevertheless, one reason for the close connection can be clearly discerned. The Confucians and Mo-ists consistently described the ideal ruler in moral and religious terms: father and mother of the people, the man of perfect virtue, the Son of Heaven. Legalism, because it rejected all appeals to religion and morality, had to find some other set of terms in which to describe and glorify the ruler. Taoism, which likewise rejected the concepts of conventional religion and morality, provided such a set. The language used by Taoism to describe the Taoist sage was therefore taken over by the Legalists and employed to describe the omnipotent ruler of the ideal Legalist state.

The Taoist sage has absolute understanding; the Legalist ruler wields absolute power. In the quality of absoluteness, they are alike. The Taoist sage rises above all conventional distinctions of right and wrong, good and evil; so does the Legalist ruler, for he is a law unto himself. The Taoist sage adopts a course of quietude and deliberately refrains from all forced or unnatural activity. The Legalist ruler, head of a vast bureaucracy, does the same, issuing orders, quietly judging the efficiency of his ministers, but refraining from any personal intervention in the actual affairs of administration; he sets up the machinery of government and then allows it to run by itself. The Taoist sage withdraws from the world to a mysterious and transcendental realm. The Legalist ruler likewise withdraws, deliberately shunning contacts with his subordinates that might breed familiarity, dwelling deep within his palace, concealing his true motives and desires, and surrounding himself with an aura of mystery and inscrutability. Like the head of a great modern corporation he sits, far removed from his countless employees, at his desk in the innermost office and quietly initials things.

Legalist thought in general, and that of Han Fei Tzu in particular, is marked by a drastically low opinion of human nature. Some scholars detect in the latter case the influence of Han Fei Tzu's teacher, Hsün Tzu, who taught that the nature of man is basically evil, though in the China of the third century B.C. one would hardly have had to sit at the feet of a philosopher to arrive at this morose conclusion. The Confucians and Mo-ists claimed that there had been better days under the sage kings of antiquity, and cited history to support their argument. Han Fei Tzu, who customarily cited history only to enlarge his catalogue of human follies and idiocies, countered that, if there had actually been peace and order in ancient times, it was not because of any moral guidance of the sages, but only because there were more goods and wealth to go around then, and fewer men to scramble for them. According to him, all attempts to educate and uplift the common people are futile, and charity is a positive sin because it robs the industrious to pamper prodigals and idlers. The ruler, to succeed, must eschew all impulses toward mercy and affection and be guided solely by enlightened self-interest. Even his own friends and relations, his own wife and children, Han Fei Tzu warned, are not to be trusted, since all for one reason or another stand to profit by his death. He must be constantly alert, constantly on his guard against deception from all quarters, trusting no one and never revealing his inner thoughts and desires. "The leper pities the king," said Han Fei Tzu, quoting an old proverb (sec. 14), and the reader may do the same.

Han Fei Tzu wrote his essays on political science for the king of Han. But it was Han's enemy and eventual destroyer, the king of Ch'in, who appreciated them and put them into practice. For over a century the state of Ch'in had been pursuing typically Legalist policies, encouraging agriculture and warfare, disciplining its people with stern laws, and conducting its foreign affairs with cold-blooded cynicism. In 221 B.C. the king of Ch'in completed his conquest of the other states and united all of China under his rule. Assuming the title of First Emperor, he set about creating the vast bureaucratic empire that Han Fei Tzu had envisioned. He abolished the last remnants of feudalism, standardized weights, measures, and the writing system, controlled the people with strict laws, suppressed the teachings of other schools of philosophy, undertook huge public works, and launched foreign wars to push back the borders of his domain—all measures either recommended by, or in keeping with the spirit of, Legalism. Finally, he built magnificent palaces and surrounded himself with the appropriate air of aloofness and mystery. But by the time of his death in 210 B.C. the dynasty was showing unmistakable signs of strain, and three years later it fell. In part it fell because of forces beyond its control—the centrifugal pull of old local loyalties, the high cost of state undertakings, the natural resistance of men to violent change. But Chinese historians have customarily blamed its downfall upon its harsh and ruthless treatment of the people, and their view is undoubtedly in part correct. Lack of mercy is the charge most often brought against Han Fei Tzu and the other Legalist philosophers, and the First Emperor, following their doctrines, seems to have seriously overestimated the amount of bullying and oppression his people would bear. As a philosophy of government, Legalism was tried and found wanting. No government in China thereafter ever attempted to apply its policies in undiluted form. But the penetrating analyses and astute advice that fill the *Han Fei Tzu* have been profitably drawn upon again and again by later rulers and political theorists, and remain of vital interest today.

The *Han Fei Tzu* is divided into 55 sections. In the

"Treatise on Literature" of the *History of the Former Han*, and other early bibliographies, it is listed under the title *Han Tzu*; the word *Fei* was added to the title much later to distinguish it from the writings of the T'ang Confucian scholar Han Yü (786–824). Most of the sections are short, concise essays on some aspect of Legalist thought, fitted with titles, and closely resembling the essays of earlier works such as the *Mo Tzu, Hsün Tzu,* or *Book of Lord Shang.* Nearly all the twelve sections in my selection are of this type. Some of the sections consist of anecdotes drawn from the historical writings or legends of late Chou times and designed to demonstrate the validity of Legalist policies by illustrations from the past, or to cast aspersions on the teachings of other schools of thought. I have included one such chapter, section 10, in my selection; there is some doubt as to whether it is actually from the hand of Han Fei Tzu himself, but it illustrates the fondness of the Legalists for elucidating their pronouncements by concrete examples from history. Two sections in my selection, sections 5 and 8, employ typical Taoist terminology, and are couched in an extremely terse, balanced style, with frequent use of rhymes, that is not typical of the work as a whole. Two other sections, not translated here, are actually cast in the form of commentaries upon passages from Lao Tzu's *Tao-te-ching.* They give the Taoist classic a purely political interpretation, Legalist with Confucian borrowings, and are probably the work of scholars of the Ch'in or early Han period. Other sections of the *Han Fei Tzu* are likewise almost certainly the work of later writers of the Legalist school; and some passages may even be part of an essay written by a scholar named Liu T'ao (d. A.D. 185) to refute Han Fei Tzu's teachings, which have somehow found their way into the text. Though there is disagreement among scholars as to just which sections are the work of Han Fei Tzu himself, I see no reason, with the exception mentioned above, to doubt the authenticity of the sections I have translated.

The fourth and third centuries B.C. saw the appearance of a body of technical literature in Chinese—treatises on divination, medicine, agriculture, logic, military science, and so forth. The *Han Fei Tzu* is actually more closely allied to this genre than to the broader philosophical works of the period. Han Fei Tzu's teacher, Hsün Tzu, wrote on such widely varied subjects as politics, warfare, ethics, esthetics, logic, and epistemology. But Han Fei Tzu and the other authors of the book which bears his name confine themselves rigidly to one subject—politics. Within the limits they set themselves, however, their treatment is exhaustive. There is hardly a problem of administration that they have not analyzed and discussed, hardly a pitfall they have not warned against. The style of the work is, on the whole, clear, concise, and polished, though metaphors are occasionally allowed to get out of hand. Its treatment is witty, trenchant, and marked by an air of sophistication and cynicism. Generations of Chinese scholars have professed to be shocked by its contents— the rejection of all moral values, the call to harshness and deceit in politics, the assertion that even one's own wife and children are not to be trusted—and have taken up their brushes to denounce it. But there has never been an age when the book was unread, and the text appears to have come down to us complete. It is one of those books that will compel attention in any age, for it deals with a problem of unchanging importance—the nature and use of power.

My translation is based on the *Han Fei Tzu chi-shih* by Ch'en Ch'i-yu (2 vols., Shanghai, 1958). In his exhaustive notes, Ch'en has drawn upon all the important studies and commentaries of earlier Chinese and Japanese scholars (his bibliography lists 89 titles), adding his own suggestions for emendation and interpretation. I have also consulted the *Han Tzu ch'ien-chieh* by Liang Ch'i-hsiung (2 vols., Peking, 1960); the Japanese translation by Uno Tetsuto in the Kokuyaku kanbun taisei series (1921), and that by Takeuchi Teruo (vol. I only, Tokyo, 1960); the English translation by W. K. Liao, *The Complete Works of Han Fei Tzu* 2 vols., London, Probsthain, 1939–59; and the partial translation of section 12 by Arthur Waley in *Three Ways of Thought in Ancient China* (London, 1939), pp. 242–47.

THE WAY OF THE RULER

(SECTION 5)

The Way is the beginning of all beings and the measure of right and wrong. Therefore the enlightened ruler holds fast to the beginning in order to understand the wellspring of all beings, and minds the measure in order to know the source of good and bad. He waits, empty and still,[1] letting names define themselves and affairs reach their own settlement. Being empty, he can comprehend the true aspect of fullness; being still, he can correct the mover.[2] Those whose duty it is to speak will come forward to name themselves; those whose duty it is to act will produce results. When names and results[3] match, the ruler need do nothing more and the true aspect of all things will be revealed.

Hence it is said: The ruler must not reveal his desires; for if he reveals his desires his ministers will put on the mask that pleases him. He must not reveal his will; for if he does so his ministers will show a different face. So it is said: Discard likes and dislikes and the ministers will show their true form; discard wisdom and wile and the ministers will watch their step. Hence, though the ruler is wise, he hatches no schemes from his wisdom, but causes all men to know

[1] Omitting the first *ling*. This section, like sec. 8 below, is distinguished by the frequent use of end rhymes.

[2] Reading *wei* for the second *chih*.

[3] Literally, "forms" or "realities." But Han Fei Tzu is discussing concrete problems of political science, i.e., do the officials really do what they say they are going to do? Does their actual performance match the title they hold?

their place. Though he has worth, he does not display it in his deeds, but observes the motives of his ministers. Though he is brave, he does not flaunt his bravery in shows of indignation, but allows his subordinates to display their valor to the full. Thus, though he discards wisdom, his rule is enlightened; though he discards worth, he achieves merit; and though he discards bravery, his state grows powerful. When the ministers stick to their posts, the hundred officials have their regular duties, and the ruler employs each according to his particular ability, this is known as the state of manifold constancy.

Hence it is said: "So still he seems to dwell nowhere at all; so empty no one can seek him out." The enlightened ruler reposes in nonaction above, and below his ministers tremble with fear.

This is the way of the enlightened ruler: he causes the wise to bring forth all their schemes, and he decides his affairs accordingly; hence his own wisdom is never exhausted. He causes the worthy to display their talents, and he employs them accordingly; hence his own worth never comes to an end. Where there are accomplishments, the ruler takes credit for their worth; where there are errors, the ministers are held responsible for the blame; hence the ruler's name never suffers. Thus, though the ruler is not worthy himself, he is the leader of the worthy; though he is not wise himself, he is the corrector of the wise. The ministers have the labor; the ruler enjoys the success. This is called the maxim of the worthy ruler.

The Way lies in what cannot be seen, its function in what cannot be known. Be empty, still, and idle, and from your place of darkness observe the defects of others. See but do not appear to see; listen but do not seem to listen; know but do not let it be known that you know. When you perceive the trend of a man's words, do not change them, do not correct them, but examine them and compare them with the results. Assign one man to each office and do not let men talk to each other, and then all will do their utmost. Hide your tracks, conceal your sources, so that your subordinates cannot trace the springs of your action. Discard wisdom, forswear ability, so that your subordinates cannot guess what you are about. Stick to your objectives and examine the results to see how they match; take hold of the handles of government carefully and grip them tightly.[4] Destroy all hope, smash all intention of wresting them from you; allow no man to covet them.

If you do not guard the door, if you do not make fast the gate, then tigers will lurk there. If you are not cautious in your undertakings, if you do not hide their true aspect, then traitors will arise. They murder their sovereign and usurp his place, and all men in fear make common cause with them: hence they are called tigers. They sit by the ruler's side and, in the service of evil ministers, spy into his secrets: hence they are called traitors. Smash their cliques, arrest their backers, shut the gate, deprive them of all hope of support, and the nation will be free of tigers. Be immeasurably great, be unfathomably deep; make certain that names and results tally, examine laws and customs, punish those who act willfully, and the state will be without traitors.

The ruler of men stands in danger of being blocked in five ways. When the ministers shut out their ruler, this is one kind of block. When they get control of the wealth and resources of the state, this is a second kind of block. When they are free to issue orders as they please, this is a third kind.

---

[4] On the two handles of government—punishment and favor—see below, sec. 7.

When they are able to do righteous deeds in their own name, this is a fourth kind. When they are able to build up their own cliques, this is a fifth kind. If the ministers shut out the ruler, then he loses the effectiveness of his position. If they control wealth and resources, he loses the means of dispensing bounty to others. If they issue orders as they please, he loses the means of command. If they are able to carry out righteous deeds in their own name, he loses his claim to enlightenment. And if they can build up cliques of their own, he loses his supporters. All these are rights that should be exercised by the ruler alone; they should never pass into the hands of his ministers.

The way of the ruler of men is to treasure stillness and reserve. Without handling affairs himself, he can recognize clumsiness or skill in others; without laying plans of his own, he knows what will bring fortune or misfortune. Hence he need speak no word, but good answers will be given him; he need exact no promises, but good works will increase. When proposals have been brought before him, he takes careful note of their content; when undertakings are well on their way, he takes careful note of the result; and from the degree to which proposals and results tally, rewards and punishments are born. Thus the ruler assigns undertakings to his various ministers on the basis of the words they speak, and assesses their accomplishments according to the way they have carried out the undertaking. When accomplishments match the undertaking, and the undertaking matches what was said about it, then he rewards the man; when these things do not match, he punishes the man. It is the way of the enlightened ruler never to allow[5] his ministers to speak words that cannot be matched by results.

[5] Supplying *te* before *ch'en*.

Man's punishment ≠ Way's punishment

The enlightened ruler in bestowing rewards is as benign as the seasonable rain; the dew of his bounty profits all men. But in doling out punishment he is as terrible as the thunder; even the holy sages cannot assuage him. The enlightened ruler is never overliberal in his rewards, never overlenient in his punishments. If his rewards are too liberal, then ministers who have won merit in the past will grow lax in their duties; and if his punishments are too lenient, then evil ministers will find it easy to do wrong. Thus if a man has truly won merit, no matter how humble and far removed he may be, he must be rewarded; and if he has truly committed error, no matter how close and dear to the ruler he may be, he must be punished. If those who are humble and far removed can be sure of reward,[6] and those close and dear to the ruler can be sure of punishment, then the former will not stint in their efforts and the latter will not grow proud.

[6] This first clause has dropped out of the text but can be restored from a quotation preserved elsewhere.

ON HAVING STANDARDS

(SECTION 6)

No state is forever strong or forever weak. If those who uphold the law are strong, the state will be strong; if they are weak, the state will be weak. King Chuang (r. 613–591) of Ch'u annexed twenty-six states and extended his territory three thousand *li*, but death called him from his altars of the soil and grain, and Ch'u in time declined. Duke Huan (r. 685–643) of Ch'i annexed thirty states and opened up his territory three thousand *li*, but death called him from his altars of the soil and grain, and Ch'i in time declined. King Chao (r. 311–279) [1] of Yen extended his domain to the Yellow River on the south, made his capital at Chi, and strengthened his defenses at Cho and Fang-ch'eng; he overran the state of Ch'i and conquered Chung-shan, until all who allied themselves with him were looked on as powerful and all who did not as insignificant; but death called him from his altars, and Yen in time declined. King An-hsi (r. 276–243) of Wei attacked Yen to save Chao,[2] seized the area east of the Yellow River, attacked and gained complete control of the regions of T'ao and Wei, dispatched troops against Ch'i, and seized the city of P'ing-lu for his private use; he attacked Han, took control of Kuan, and won victory at the Ch'i River; in the campaign at Sui-yang the Ch'u army ran from him in exhaustion, and in the campaign at Ts'ai and Chao-ling the Ch'u army was crushed; his troops marched to the four quarters of the

---

[1] The text erroneously reads King Hsiang.
[2] The text erroneously reads "attacked Chao to save Yen."

world and his might overawed the cap-and-girdle states;[3] but after King An-hsi died, Wei in time declined.

Thus, under Chuang and Huan the states of Ch'u and Ch'i became dictators; and under Chao and An-hsi the states of Yen and Wei were strong. But now all of them have become doomed countries, because their ministers and officials pursue only what brings chaos and never what brings order. Their states have already fallen into disorder and weakness, and yet the ministers and officials disregard the laws and seek private gain in dealings with foreign powers. One might as well carry bundles of kindling to put out a fire with—the chaos and weakness can only increase.

In our present age he who can put an end to private scheming and make men uphold the public law will see his people secure and his state well ordered; he who can block selfish pursuits and enforce the public law will see his armies growing stronger and his enemies weakening. Find men who have a clear understanding of what is beneficial to the nation and a feeling for the system of laws and regulations, and place them in charge of the lesser officials; then the ruler can never be deceived by lies and falsehoods. Find men who have a clear understanding of what is beneficial to the nation and the judgment to weigh issues properly, and put them in charge of foreign affairs; then the ruler can never be deceived in his relations with the other powers of the world.

Now if able men are selected for promotion on the basis of reputation alone, then the officials will disregard the ruler and seek only the good will of their associates and subordinates. If appointments to office are controlled by cliques, then men will work only to establish profitable connections and will not

[3] I. e., the states in which Chinese dress was worn.

try to achieve office by regular routes. In such cases, official posts will never be filled by able men, and the state will fall into disorder. If rewards are handed out on the basis of good report alone, and punishments on the basis of slander, then men who covet rewards and fear punishment will abandon the public interest and pursue only private schemes, banding together to further each other's interests. If men forget who their sovereign is and enter into association with foreign powers in order to further the interests of their own group, then subordinates will be of little aid to their superiors. If the groups are large and their allies numerous, so that a single clique embraces men both inside and outside the state, then, though its members commit a glaring fault, they will find plentiful means to conceal it. As a result, truly loyal ministers will face peril and death even though they are guilty of no fault; while evil ministers will enjoy safety and profit which they have done nothing to deserve. If loyal ministers, though guiltless, still face peril and death, then good officials will go into hiding; and if evil ministers, though without merit, enjoy safety and profit, then corrupt officials will come to the fore. This is the beginning of downfall.

In such cases, the officials will turn their backs on law, seeking only to establish weighty personal connections and making light of public duty. Numbers of them will flock to the gates of powerful men, but none will appear in the ruler's court. They will lay a hundred plans for the advancement of private family interests, but give not one thought to how the ruler should order his state. Thus, although there are plenty of men attached to the administration, they will not be the kind who will honor their ruler; though all the official posts are filled, none who fill them will be the kind who can be entrusted with affairs of state. So, although the sovereign holds the title of ruler of men, he will in fact be a pawn of the ministerial families.

Therefore I say:[4] There are no men in the court of a doomed state. When I say there are no men, I do not mean that the actual number of men at court is any less than usual. But the powerful families seek only to benefit each other and not to enrich the state; the high ministers seek only to honor each other and not to honor their sovereign; and the petty officials cling to their stipends and work to make influential friends instead of attending to their duties. And the reason such a state of affairs has come about is that the ruler does not make important decisions on the basis of law, but puts faith in whatever his subordinates do.

A truly enlightened ruler uses the law to select men for him; he does not choose them himself. He uses the law to weigh their merits; he does not attempt to judge them for himself. Hence men of true worth will not be able to hide their talents, nor spoilers to gloss over their faults. Men cannot advance on the basis of praise alone, nor be driven from court by calumny. Then there will be a clear understanding of values between the ruler and his ministers, and the state can be easily governed. But only if the ruler makes use of law can he hope to achieve this.

When a man of true worth becomes a minister, he faces north before the sovereign, presents tokens of his allegiance,[5] and banishes from his mind the thought of all other loyalties. If he serves at court, he does not venture to excuse himself

---

[4] Literally, "Your servant says," suggesting that this was originally a memorial to some ruler, probably the king of Han.

[5] Ritually prescribed gifts presented upon entering the service of a ruler Chinese rulers always sat facing south when holding audience.

because of the lowliness of the post assigned him; if he serves in the army, he does not dare to shirk danger. He follows the lead of his superiors and obeys the laws of his sovereign; with empty mind he awaits orders and does not question whether they are right or wrong. Thus, though he has a mouth, he never uses it to speak for private advantage; though he has eyes, he never employs them to spy private gain; in all things he is under the control of his superior. A minister may be compared to a hand, which reaches up to serve the head or reaches down to tend the foot; its duty is to relieve the body from heat or cold and, when swords threaten,[6] it dare not fail to strike out at them. For his part, the ruler must never make selfish use of his wise ministers or able men. So the people are never tempted to go beyond their communities to form friendships, nor need they worry about what happens a hundred *li* away. Honorable and humble do not get in each other's way, and stupid and wise find their proper place. This is the perfection of good government.

Men who are contemptuous of ranks and stipends, quick to discard their posts and abandon the state in search of another sovereign, I would not call upright. Those who propound false doctrines and controvert the law, who defy their sovereign or oppose him with strong censure, I would not call loyal. Those who practice charity and dole out benefits in order to win over their subordinates and make a name for themselves, I would not call benevolent. Those who withdraw from the world, live in retirement, and employ their wits to spread false slander against their superiors,[7] I would not call righteous.

---

[6] Omitting the *ju*, which is either superfluous or the remnant of a clause that has dropped out.

[7] Following Ch'en Ch'i-yu, who amends *tso* to *cha* and supplies *chih* above it.

Those who devote all their time to establishing favorable relations with the princes of other states, impoverishing their own state in the process, and who, when they see the moment of crisis approaching, attempt to intimidate their sovereign by saying, "Only through me can friendly relations be established with So-and-so; only through me can So-and-so's anger be appeased!", until the ruler comes to believe in them and entrusts all state affairs to their decision; who lower the name of the ruler in order to enhance their own eminence, who raid the resources of the state in order to benefit their own families— such men I would not call wise.

Deeds such as these prevail in a dangerous age, but were precluded by the laws of the former kings. The law of the former kings says, "Ministers shall not wield the instruments of authority nor dispense benefits, but follow the commands of the king; none shall do evil, but uphold the king's path." In antiquity the people of a well-ordered age upheld the public law and renounced private schemes, concentrated their attention upon one goal and their actions upon one object, and together awaited the charge that was laid upon them.

If the ruler of men tries to keep a personal check on all the various offices of his government, he will find the day too short and his energies insufficient. Moreover if the ruler uses his eyes, his subordinates will try to prettify what he sees; if he uses his ears, they will try to embellish what he hears; and if he uses his mind, they will be at him with endless speeches. The former kings, knowing that these three faculties would not suffice, accordingly set aside their own abilities; instead they relied upon law and policy, and took care to see that rewards and punishments were correctly apportioned. Since they held fast to the essential point, their legal codes were simple and yet inviolable, and alone they exercised control over all within the four seas. Even the cleverest men could find no opening for their falsehoods, the glibbest talkers no audience for their sophistries, and evil and deceit were left without a foothold. Though a thousand miles from the ruler's side, men did not dare say anything different from what they had said in his presence; though courtiers in the palace, they did not dare to conceal good or gloss over evil. Courtiers and officials flocked to the service of their sovereign, each diligently attending to his own duties, and none dared overstep his position. Affairs of government were not pressing[8] and time was left to spare. The way in which the ruler relied upon his position made it so.

The process by which ministers invade the rights of their sovereign is as gradual as the shifting of the contours of the landscape. Little by little they cause him to lose his sense of direction, until he is facing east where before he faced west, and yet he is unaware of the change. Hence the former kings set up south-pointing markers to determine the direction of sunrise and sunset. In the same way, an enlightened ruler will make certain that the ambitions of his ministers do not roam beyond the bounds of the law, and that they do not go about dispensing favors even though such acts may be within the law. They are permitted to make no move that is not in accord with law. Laws are the means of prohibiting error and ruling out selfish motives;[9] strict penalties are the means of enforcing orders and disciplining inferiors. Authority should never reside in two places;[10] the power of decree should never be open to joint use. If authority and power are shared with

[8] Emending *tsu* to *ts'u* in accordance with the suggestion of Ch'en Ch'i-yu; but the meaning is very doubtful.

[9] Amending *ling* to *chin* and omitting *yu* in accordance with the suggestion of Ch'en Ch'i-yu.

[10] Reading *erh* instead of *tai*.

others, then all manner of abuse will become rife. If law does not command respect, then all the ruler's actions will be endangered. If penalties are not enforced, then evil will never be surmounted.

Though a skilled carpenter is capable of judging a straight line with his eye alone, he will always take his measurements with a rule; though a man of superior wisdom is capable of handling affairs by native wit alone, he will always look to the laws of the former kings for guidance. Stretch the plumb line, and crooked wood can be planed straight; apply the level, and bumps and hollows can be shaved away; balance the scales, and heavy and light can be adjusted; get out the measuring jars, and discrepancies of quantity can be corrected. In the same way one should use laws to govern the state, disposing of all matters on their basis alone.

The law no more makes exceptions for men of high station than the plumb line bends to accommodate a crooked place in the wood. What the law has decreed the wise man cannot dispute nor the brave man venture to contest. When faults are to be punished, the highest minister cannot escape; when good is to be rewarded, the lowest peasant must not be passed over. Hence, for correcting the faults of superiors, chastising the misdeeds of subordinates, restoring order, exposing error, checking excess, remedying evil, and unifying the standards of the people, nothing can compare to law. For putting fear into the officials, awing the people, wiping out wantonness and sloth, and preventing lies and deception, nothing can compare to penalties. If penalties are heavy, men dare not use high position to abuse the humble; if laws are clearly defined, superiors will be honored and their rights will not be invaded. If they are honored and their rights are inviolable, then the ruler will be strong and will hold fast to what is essential. Hence the former kings held laws in high esteem and handed them down to posterity. Were the ruler of men to discard law and follow his private whim, then all distinction between high and low would cease to exist.

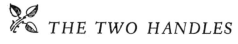# THE TWO HANDLES

(SECTION 7)

The enlightened ruler controls his ministers by means of two
handles alone. The two handles are punishment and favor.
What do I mean by punishment and favor? To inflict mutila-
tion and death on men is called punishment; to bestow honor
and reward is called favor. Those who act as ministers fear
the penalties and hope to profit by the rewards. Hence, if the
ruler wields his punishments and favors, the ministers will
fear his sternness and flock to receive his benefits. But the
evil ministers of the age are different. They cajole the ruler
into letting them inflict punishment themselves on men they
hate and bestow rewards on men they like. Now if the ruler
of men does not insist upon reserving to himself the right to
dispense profit in the form of rewards and show his sternness
in punishments, but instead hands them out on the advice of
his ministers, then the people of the state will all fear the
ministers and hold the ruler in contempt, will flock to the
ministers and desert the ruler. This is the danger that arises
when the ruler loses control of punishments and favors.

The tiger is able to overpower the dog because of his claws
and teeth, but if he discards his claws and teeth and lets the
dog use them, then on the contrary he will be overpowered
by the dog. In the same way the ruler of men uses punishments and favors to control his ministers, but if he discards his
punishments and favors and lets his ministers employ them,
then on the contrary he will find himself in the control of his
ministers.

T'ien Ch'ang petitioned the ruler for various titles and stipends, which he then dispensed to the other ministers, and used an extra large measure in doling out grain to the common people. In this way the ruler, Duke Chien, lost the exclusive right to dispense favors, and it passed into T'ien Ch'ang's hands instead. That was how Duke Chien came to be assassinated.[1]

Tzu-han said to the ruler of Sung, "Since the people all delight in rewards and gifts, you should bestow them yourself; but since they hate punishments and death sentences, I beg to be allowed to dispense these for you." Thereupon the ruler of Sung gave up the exclusive right to hand out penalties and it passed into the hands of Tzu-han. That was how the ruler of Sung came to be intimidated.[2]

T'ien Ch'ang got to bestow favors as he pleased, and Duke Chien was assassinated; Tzu-han got to hand out punishments as he pleased, and the ruler of Sung was intimidated. Hence, if the ministers of the present age are permitted to share in the right to hand out punishments and favors, the rulers of the time will put themselves in greater peril than Duke Chien and the lord of Sung. Invariably when rulers are intimidated, assassinated, obstructed, or forced into the shade, it has always come about because they relinquished the rights to administer punishment and favor to their ministers, and thus brought about their own peril and downfall.

If the ruler of men wishes to put an end to evil-doing, then

---

[1] In 481 B.C. T'ien Ch'ang, a high minister of Ch'i, assassinated the ruler of Ch'i, Duke Chien. Earlier, T'ien Ch'ang was said to have won the support of the people by using a larger-than-standard measure in doling out grain to the people, but the standard measure when collecting taxes in grain. See *Tso chuan*, Duke Chao, 3d yr.

[2] The incident to which Han Fei Tzu is referring here is otherwise unknown.

he must be careful to match up names and results, that is to say, words and deeds.[3] The ministers come forward to present their proposals; the ruler assigns them tasks on the basis of their words, and then concentrates on demanding the accomplishment of the task. If the accomplishment fits the task, and the task fits the words, then he bestows reward; but if they do not match, he doles out punishment. Hence, if one of the ministers comes forward with big words but produces only small accomplishments, the ruler punishes him, not because the accomplishments are small, but because they do not match the name that was given to the undertaking. Likewise, if one of the ministers comes forward with small words but produces great accomplishments, he too is punished, not because the ruler is displeased at great accomplishments, but because he considers the discrepancy in the name given to the undertaking to be a fault too serious to be outweighed by great accomplishments.

Once in the past Marquis Chao of Han got drunk and fell asleep. The keeper of the royal hat, seeing that the marquis was cold, laid a robe over him. When the marquis awoke, he was pleased and asked his attendants, "Who covered me with a robe?" "The keeper of the hat," they replied. The marquis thereupon punished both the keeper of the royal hat and the keeper of the royal robe. He punished the keeper of the robe for failing to do his duty, and the keeper of the hat for overstepping his office. It was not that he did not dislike the cold, but he considered the trespass of one official upon the duties of another to be a greater danger than cold.

Hence an enlightened ruler, in handling his ministers, does not permit them to gain merit by overstepping their offices, or to speak words that do not tally with their actions. Those who

---

[3] Reading *yü* instead of *yi*.

overstep their offices are condemned to die; those whose words and actions do not tally are punished. If the ministers are made to stick to their proper duties and speak only what is just, then they will be unable to band together in cliques to work for each other's benefit.

The ruler of men has two worries: if he employs only worthy men, then his ministers will use the appeal to worthiness as a means to intimidate him; on the other hand, if he promotes men in an arbitrary manner, then state affairs will be bungled and will never reach a successful conclusion. Hence, if the ruler shows a fondness for worth, his ministers will all strive to put a pleasing façade on their actions in order to satisfy his desires. In such a case, they will never show their true colors, and if they never show their true colors, then the ruler will have no way to distinguish the able from the worthless. Because the king of Yüeh admired valor, many of his subjects defied death; because King Ling of Ch'u liked slim waists, his state was full of half-starved people on diets. Because Duke Huan of Ch'i was jealous and loved his ladies in waiting, Shu-tiao castrated himself in order to be put in charge of the harem; because the duke was fond of unusual food, Yi-ya steamed his son's head and offered it to the duke. Because Tzu-k'uai of Yen admired worthy men, Tzu-chih insisted that he would not accept the throne even if it were offered to him.[4]

---

[4] In his later years Duke Huan (r. 685–643 B.C.) of Ch'i relied heavily upon Shu-tiao and Yi-ya, two evil ministers who were said to have ingratiated themselves with the duke in the unpleasant manner mentioned. As a result, when the duke died, the court was torn by party strife. (See below, p. 68.) In 316 B.C. King K'uai of Yen, hoping to imitate the sages of antiquity who were said to have offered their thrones to worthy men, offered his own throne to his minister Tzu-chih. Contrary to the king's expectation, Tzu-chih accepted it, became ruler, and brought the state close to ruin.

Thus, if the ruler reveals what he dislikes, his ministers will be careful to disguise their motives; if he shows what he likes, his ministers will feign abilities they do not have. In short, if he lets his desires be known, he gives his ministers a clue as to what attitude they had best assume.

Hence Tzu-chih, by playing the part of a worthy, was able to snatch power from his sovereign; Shu-tiao and Yi-ya, by catering to the ruler's desires, were able to invade his authority. As a result, Tzu-k'uai died in the chaos that ensued, and Duke Huan was left unburied for so long that maggots came crawling out the door of his death chamber.

What caused this? It is an example of the calamity that comes when the ruler reveals his feelings to his ministers. As far as the feelings of the ministers go, they do not necessarily love their ruler; they serve him only in the hope of substantial gain. Now if the ruler of men does not hide his feelings and conceal his motives, but instead gives his ministers a foothold by which they may invade his rights, then they will have no difficulty in doing what Tzu-chih and T'ien Ch'ang did. Hence it is said: Do away with likes, do away with hates, and the ministers will show their true colors. And when the ministers have shown their true colors, the ruler of men will never be deceived.[5]

[5] Reading *jen* instead of *ta*.

 *WIELDING POWER* [1]

(SECTION 8)

Both Heaven [Nature] and man have their fixed destinies. Fragrant aromas and delicate flavors, rich wine and fat meat delight the palate but sicken the body. Fair lineaments and pearly teeth warm the heart but waste the spirit. Therefore renounce riot and excess, for only then can you keep your health unharmed.

Do not let your power be seen; be blank and actionless. Government reaches to the four quarters, but its source is in the center. The sage holds to the source and the four quarters come to serve him. In emptiness he awaits them, and they spontaneously do what is needed. When all within the four seas have been put in their proper places, he sits in darkness to observe the light. When those to his left and right have taken their places, he opens the gate to face the world. He changes nothing, alters nothing, but acts with the two handles of reward and punishment, acts and never ceases: this is what is called walking the path of principle.

Things have their proper place, talents their proper use. When all are in their proper place, then superior and inferior may be free from action. Let the cock herald the dawn, let the cat catch rats. When each exercises his ability, the ruler need do nothing. If the ruler tries to excel, then nothing will go

[1] In this chapter, Han Fei Tzu borrows the laconic language of Taoist quietism to express his political philosophy, using short, neatly balanced phrases with frequent end rhymes. Because of the deliberately arcane mode of expression he employs, commentators disagree at many points on exactly what he is saying.

right. If he boasts of an eye for the abilities of others, he will invite deceit among his subordinates. If he is lenient and fond of sparing lives, his subordinates will impose upon his kind nature. If superior and inferior try to change roles, the state will never be ordered.

Use the single Way and make names the head of it. When names are correct, things stay in place; when names are twisted, things shift about. Hence the sage holds to unity in stillness; he lets names define themselves and affairs reach their own settlement. He does not reveal his nature, and his subordinates are open and upright. He assigns them tasks according to their ability and lets them settle[2] things for themselves; he hands out rewards according to the results and lets them raise their own station. He establishes the standard, abides by it, and lets all things settle themselves. On the basis of names he makes his appointments, and where the name is not clear, he looks to the actual achievement it applies to. According to how achievement and name tally, he dispenses the reward or punishment deserved. When rewards and punishments are certain to be handed out, then subordinates will bare their true nature.

Attend diligently to these matters, await the decree of Heaven, do not lose hold of the vital point, and you may become a sage. Discard wisdom and wile, for, if you do not, you will find it hard to remain constant. When the people use wisdom and wile, they bring grave danger to themselves; when the ruler uses them, his state faces peril and destruction. Follow the way of Heaven, reflect on the principle behind human affairs; investigate, examine, and compare these things, and when you come to the end, begin again. Be empty, quiet, and retiring; never put yourself forward. All the worries of

---

[2] Reading *ting* instead of *shih*.

the ruler come about because he tries to be like others. Trust others but never be like them, and then the myriad people will follow you as one man.

The Way is vast and great and without form; its Power is clear and orderly and extends everywhere. Since it extends to all living beings, they may use it proportionately; but, though all things flourish through it, it does not rest among things. The Way pervades all affairs here below. Therefore examine and obey the decrees of Heaven[3] and live and die at the right time; compare names, differentiate events, comprehend their unity, and identify yourself with the Way's true nature.

Thus it is said: The Way does not identify itself with the myriad beings; its Power does not identify itself with the yin and yang, any more than a scale identifies itself with heaviness or lightness, a plumb line with bumps and hollows, a reed organ with dampness or dryness,[4] or a ruler with his ministers. All these [the myriad beings, the yin and yang, heaviness and lightness, etc.] are products of the Way; but the Way itself is never plural—therefore it is called a unity. For this reason the enlightened ruler prizes solitariness, which is the characteristic of the Way. The ruler and his ministers do not follow the same way. The ministers name their proposals, the ruler holds fast to the name, and the ministers come forward with results. When names and results match, then superior and inferior will achieve harmony.

The way to listen to the words of the ministers is to take the statements that come from them and compare them with the powers that have been invested in them. Therefore you must

[3] Reading *t'ien* instead of *erh*. In Taoist terminology, Heaven is synonymous with the Way, or Tao.

[4] A kind of reed musical instrument whose pitch was said to remain unaffected by changes of humidity; it could therefore be used to set the pitch for other instruments.

examine names carefully in order to establish ranks, clarify duties in order to distinguish worth. This is the way to listen to the words of others: be silent as though in a drunken stupor. Say to yourself: Lips! teeth! do not be the first to move; lips! teeth! be thicker, be clumsier than ever! Let others say their piece—I will gain knowledge thereby.

Though right and wrong swarm about him, the ruler does not argue with them. Be empty, still, inactive, for this is the true nature of the Way. Study, compare, and see what matches, for this will reveal how much has been accomplished. Compare with concrete results; check against empty assertions. Where the root and base of the affair are unshaken, there will be no error in movement or stillness. Whether you move or remain still, transform all though inaction. If you show delight, your affairs will multiply; if you show hatred, resentment will be born. Therefore discard both delight and hatred and with an empty mind become the abode of the Way.

The ruler does not try to work side by side with his people, and they accordingly respect the dignity of his position. He does not try to tell others what to do, but leaves them to do things by themselves. Tightly he bars his inner door, and from his room looks out into the courtyard; he has provided the rules and yardsticks, so that all things know their place.[5] Those who merit reward are rewarded; those who deserve punishment are punished. Reward and punishment follow the deed; each man brings them upon himself. Therefore, whether the result is pleasant or hateful, who dares to question it? When compass and rule have marked out one corner of truth, the other three corners will become evident of themselves.

If the ruler is not godlike in his isolation, his subordinates

[5] Omitting *ts'an* and reading *chih* (to know) in place of the present *chih*.

will find ways to move him. If his management of affairs is not impartial, they will guess at his inclinations. Be like Heaven, be like earth, and all coils will be untangled. Be like Heaven, be like earth; then who will be close to you, who will be distant? He who can model himself on Heaven and earth may be called a sage.

Would you order the affairs of the palace? Delegate them and be intimate with no one. Would you order outside affairs? Appoint one man to each office. Let no one do as he pleases, and never permit men to change office or to hold two offices at the same time. Take warning when there are many men gathered at the gates of the high ministers! The height of good government is to allow your subordinates no means of taking advantage of you. Make certain that name and result match, and then the people will stick to their posts. If you discard this and look for some other method to rule, you will win the name of one who is profoundly deluded; wily men will only increase, and evil ministers fill your ranks. Hence it is said: Never enrich a man to the point where he can afford to turn against you;[6] never ennoble a man to the point where he becomes a threat; never put all your trust in a single man and thereby lose your state.

When the shin grows stouter than the thigh, it is hard to run; when the ruler loses his godlike qualities, tigers prowl behind him. If the ruler fails to take notice of them, then he and his ministers, who should be tigers themselves, become as impotent as dogs. If the ruler fails to check the danger, then the dogs will continue to increase in number; the tigers will form a band and assassinate their master. A ruler who has no ministers—how can he keep possession of a state? Let the ruler apply the laws, and the greatest tigers will tremble; let

[6] Reading *erh* instead of *tai*.

him apply punishments, and the greatest tigers will grow docile. If laws and punishments are justly applied, then tigers will be transformed into men again and revert to their true form.[7]

If you wish to govern the state, you must make certain to destroy conclaves; if you do not do so, they will only grow more numerous. If you wish to govern the land, you must make certain that your bestowals pass into the right hands; if you do not do so, then unruly men will come seeking gain. If you grant what they seek, you will be lending a battle-ax to your enemies; this you must not do, for it will only be used against you.

The Yellow Emperor used to say, "Superior and inferior fight a hundred battles a day." The subordinates hide their private desires and see what they can get from the ruler; the ruler employs his standards and measures to weigh what they are up to. Thus the standards and measures that are set up are the ruler's treasures; and the parties and cliques that are formed are the ministers' treasures. The only reason the ministers do not assassinate their sovereign is that their parties and cliques are not strong enough. Hence, if the ruler loses an inch, his subordinates gain a yard.

The ruler who knows how to govern his state does not let his cities grow too large; the ruler who understands the Way does not enrich the powerful families[8] nor ennoble his ministers. Were he to enrich and ennoble them, they would turn about and try to overthrow him. Guard against danger, fear peril, make haste to designate your heir, and misfortune will have no means to arise.

---

[7] There are various theories on the symbolic meaning of the tigers and dogs in this paragraph, depending upon which the interpretation of the passage differs considerably. I have followed that of T'ao Hung-ch'ing.

[8] Reading *chün* instead of *ch'en* and *fu* instead of *kuei*.

In ferreting out evil within the palace and controlling it outside, you yourself must hold fast to your standards and measurements. Whittle away from those who have too much, enhance those who have too little, but let the taking and the giving be according to measure. Never allow men to form cliques or join together to deceive their superiors. Let your whittling be as gradual as the slimming moon, your enhancing like a slow-spreading heat. Simplify the laws and be cautious in the use of penalties but, where punishments are called for, make certain they are carried out. Never loosen your bow, or you will find two cocks in a single roost, squawking in fierce rivalry. When wildcat and wolf break into the fold, the sheep are not likely to increase. When one house has two venerables, its affairs will never prosper. When husband and wife both give orders, the children are at a loss to know which one to obey.

The ruler of men must prune his trees from time to time and not let them grow too thick for, if they do, they will block his gate; while the gates of private men are crowded with visitors, the ruler's courts will stand empty, and he will be shut in and encircled. He must prune his trees from time to time and not let them obstruct the path for, if they do, they will impinge upon his dwelling. He must prune his trees from time to time and not let the branches grow larger than the trunk for, if they do, they will not be able to bear up under the spring wind, and will do injury to the heart of the tree. When cadet houses become too numerous, the royal family will face anxiety and grief. The way to prevent this is to prune your trees from time to time and not let the branches grow too luxurious. If the trees are pruned from time to time, cliques and parties will be broken up. Dig them up from the roots, and then the trees cannot spread. Fill up the pools, and do not let water collect in them.[9] Search out the hearts of others, seize their power from them. The ruler himself should possess the power, wielding it like lightning or like thunder.

[9] Omitting *hsiung* and reading *yen* for *ch'ing* in accordance with the suggestion of Ch'en Ch'i-yu. The language of these last two paragraphs is so extravagantly metaphorical that it presents difficulties of interpretation at numerous points.

THE EIGHT VILLAINIES

There are eight strategies which ministers customarily employ to work their villainy. The first is called "Making use of his bedfellows." What do I mean by this? The ruler is easily beguiled by lovely women and charming boys, by all those who can fawn and play at love. They wait for the time when he is enjoying his ease, take advantage of the moment when he is sated with food and wine, and ask for anything they desire, for they know that by this trick their requests are sure to be heeded. The ministers therefore ply them in the palace with gold and jewels and employ them to delude the ruler. This is what I mean by making use of his bedfellows.

The second is called "Making use of his attendants." What do I mean by this? Jesters and entertainers, attendants and favorites of the ruler—men such as these cry "Yes, yes!" before he has given an order, "At once, at once!" before he has commanded them; they guess his desire before he knows it himself, watch his face and observe his expression to divine what is in his mind. In unison they step forward, in unison they retire, all of them answering and responding in a single rote, in identical phrases, so that they may move the mind of the ruler. The ministers therefore ply them in the palace with gold, jewels, baubles, and precious things, and on the outside do forbidden favors for them, employing them to bend the ruler to their desires. This is what I mean by making use of his attendants.

The third is called "Making use of his elders and kin."

What does this mean? The ruler feels close affection for his kin of the cadet families and for the princes of the blood, and consults with the elder statesmen and courtiers when he lays his plans. Hence when such men combine to urge some proposal, the ruler is certain to listen. The ministers therefore ingratiate themselves with the princes and members of the cadet families by presenting them with musicians and waiting women, and win over the elder statesmen and courtiers with fine words; they then propose various undertakings which, they assure them, when brought to successful conclusion, will bring rewards and advancement for all. In this way they delight the hearts of these men and persuade them to act against their ruler. This is what I mean by making use of his elders and kin.

The fourth is called "Encouraging baleful pursuits." What does this mean? Rulers love to beautify their palaces, terraces, and pools, to surround themselves with attractive attendants and fine dogs and horses for their amusement, though such pursuits are baleful to the ruler's welfare. The ministers therefore exhaust the energies of the people in constructing beautiful palaces, terraces, and pools, and demand heavy taxes from them to provide attractive attendants and fine dogs and horses, in order to delight the ruler and bring disorder to his mind, indulge his desires and exact some private gain in the process. This is what I mean by encouraging baleful pursuits.

The fifth is called "Making use of the people." What do I mean by this? Ministers often distribute funds in order to gratify the people, and hand out small favors in order to win the hearts of the commoners, until eventually everyone in both court and countryside is praising them alone. Thus they come to overshadow their ruler and are able to do as they please. This is what I mean by making use of the people.

The sixth is called "Making use of fluent speakers." What does this mean? The ruler, because of the nature of his up-bringing, has usually been cut off from ordinary conversation, and has seldom had an opportunity to listen to debates, and he is accordingly apt to be particularly susceptible to persuasive speaking. The ministers therefore search about for rhetoricians from other states or patronize the most able speakers in their own state, and employ them to plead their special cause. With clever and elegant phrases, fluent and compelling words, such men draw the ruler on with prospects of gain, terrify him with predictions of hazard, and completely overwhelm him with their empty preachments. This is what I mean by making use of fluent speakers.

The seventh is called "Making use of authority and might." What do I mean by this? Rulers sometimes believe that the officials and common people are capable of wielding authority and might, and hence whatever the officials and common people approve of, they approve of too; and whatever the officials and common people condemn, they condemn also. Ministers therefore gather bands of armed men around them and support knights who are willing to die in their cause, in order to make a show of their might. They make it plain that whoever works in their interest will profit, while whoever does not will die, and in this way they manage to intimidate the lesser officials and common people and further their own interests. This is what I mean by making use of authority and might.

The eighth is called "Making use of the surrounding states." What do I mean by this? It is customary with a ruler that, if his state is small, he will do the bidding of larger states, and if his army is weak, he will stand in fear of stronger armies. When the larger states come with demands, the small state must consent; when strong armies appear, the weak army must submit. The ministers therefore double the taxes, empty the coffers, and exhaust the state in the service of the great powers, and then make use of their influence with foreign powers in their efforts to mislead the ruler. The worst of them may even call out their private troops and gather them menacingly on the border[1] in order to enforce their will within the state, while even the less evil ones will from time to time call in envoys from abroad in order to disquiet the ruler and fill him with terror. This is what I mean by making use of the surrounding states.

All these eight strategies are the means by which ministers work their villainy, obstruct and terrorize the rulers of the day, and deprive them of what they should possess. One must not fail to examine them closely!

In dealing with those who share his bed, the enlightened ruler may enjoy their beauty but should not listen to their special pleas or let them come with personal requests. In dealing with his attendants, he should hold them personally responsible for their words and not allow them to speak out of turn. In dealing with his kin and elder statesmen, though he heeds their words, he should be careful to hand out the appropriate punishments or promotions afterwards, and should not let them advance to offices arbitrarily. As regards the buildings and possessions that delight and amuse the ruler, he should make certain that they are constructed and produced only on his order; the officials should never be permitted to present them as they please in an effort to ingratiate themselves with him.[2] As regards the dispensing of favors and charity, all orders to disburse emergency funds or to open up

---

[1] As though waiting to be joined by troops from abroad.

[2] The text appears to be corrupt. I omit the *shan-t'ui*.

the granaries for the relief of the people must come from the ruler; he should never allow his ministers to dole out charity on their own. As regards speeches and debates, he should be careful to discover the true ability of those whom the flatterers praise, and find out the true faults of those whom the slanderers denounce, and not allow the officials to plead on each other's behalf. In dealing with heroes and fighting men, the ruler should never hand out unduly large rewards to men who have won distinction in the army, and never pardon the offense of men who have taken up arms in a private quarrel. He must not allow the officials to use their funds to build up their own soldiery. As to the requests and demands of the feudal lords of other states, if they are lawful, he should grant them; if not, he should reject them.

When people speak of a lost ruler, they do not mean that he no longer holds possession of the state; he still holds possession of it, but it is no longer in any sense his own. A ruler who allows his ministers to use their foreign connections to seize control of internal affairs is lost. If he heeds the demands of the great powers in an effort to save himself, then he will face downfall even sooner than if he does not heed them. Therefore he refuses to heed them. His ministers, knowing that he will not heed them, no longer try to make bargains with the other feudal lords; and the other feudal lords, knowing that he will not heed them, no longer cooperate with the efforts of the ministers to dupe their own ruler.[3]

The enlightened ruler assigns posts and hands out titles and stipends as a means of promoting men of worth and talent and encouraging men of achievement. Hence it is said that men of worth and talent should receive generous stipends and be as-

---

[3] The text and interpretation of this last sentence are very doubtful. I have followed the emendation and interpretation of Wang Wei.

signed to high offices, and men of great achievement should have honorable titles and obtain rich rewards. Appoint the worthy to office by weighing their ability; hand out stipends by judging the amount of merit won. If this is done, then worthy men will not pretend to greater ability than they have in order to seek service with their ruler; men of merit will delight in carrying out their tasks; and all undertakings will reach a successful conclusion.

But rulers nowadays do not do this. They do not look to see who is worthy and unworthy or discuss who has achieved merit or worked hard; instead they employ those who have influence with the other feudal lords, or heed the private pleading of their attendants. The ruler's kinsmen and elder statesmen beg titles and stipends from the ruler and then sell them to their subordinates in order to gain wealth and profit and create a party of supporters for themselves. Hence men who have sufficient money and influence may buy posts for themselves and become honored, and those who have friends among the ruler's attendants may make use of their special pleading to win important positions. Ministers who have shown real merit and effort count for nothing, and the assignment of posts and duties proceeds on a wholly erroneous basis. Hence we find officials stealing posts to which they have no right and intriguing with foreign powers, neglecting their duties and cultivating men of wealth.[4] As a result, men of real worth become disgusted and cease to exert themselves, and men of merit grow lax and careless in their jobs. This is the mark of a doomed state!

[4] Reversing the order of *ts'ai ch'in.*

 *THE TEN FAULTS*

These are the ten faults:

1. To practice petty loyalty and thereby betray a larger loyalty.

2. To fix your eye on a petty gain and thereby lose a larger one.

3. To behave in a base and willful manner and show no courtesy to the other feudal lords, thereby bringing about your own downfall.

4. To give no ear to government affairs but long only for the sound of music, thereby plunging yourself into distress.

5. To be greedy, perverse, and too fond of profit, thereby opening the way to the destruction of the state and your own demise.

6. To become infatuated with women musicians and disregard state affairs, thereby inviting the disaster of national destruction.

7. To leave the palace for distant travels, despising the remonstrances of your ministers, which leads to grave peril for yourself.

8. To fail to heed your loyal ministers when you are at fault, insisting upon having your own way, which will in time destroy your good reputation and make you a laughing stock of others.

9. To take no account of internal strength but rely solely upon your allies abroad, which places the state in grave danger of dismemberment.

10. To ignore the demands of courtesy, though your state is small, and fail to learn from the remonstrances of your ministers, acts which lead to the downfall of your line.

1. What do I mean by petty loyalty? Long ago, when King Kung of Ch'u fought with Duke Li of Chin at Yen-ling, the Ch'u army was defeated and King Kung was wounded in the eye.[1] When the battle was at its fiercest the Ch'u commander of the army, Tzu-fan, grew thirsty and called for a drink. His page Ku-yang came forward with a flagon of wine and presented it to him. "Get away from me!" said Tzu-fan. "That's wine you have!" But Ku-yang insisted it was not wine, until Tzu-fan finally accepted it and drank it. Tzu-fan was the kind of man who is so fond of wine that, once he had tasted it, he could not stop until he had gotten drunk. Meanwhile the battle came to an end and King Kung, hoping to resume it again the next day, sent an order summoning his commander Tzu-fan, but Tzu-fan excused himself, saying that he had a pain in his heart. King Kung mounted his carriage and went in person to see Tzu-fan but, when he entered the curtains of Tzu-fan's tent and smelled the wine fumes, he turned about and left. "Even I myself was wounded in today's battle," he said. "And yet my commander, whom I most relied on, is drunk like this! He brings destruction to the sacred altars of the state of Ch'u and has no pity upon my men. I will not fight again." With this he withdrew his armies from the field and left, beheading Tzu-fan in punishment for the terrible crime he had committed.

Thus, when the page Ku-yang presented the wine, he had no thought of enmity for Tzu-fan. His heart was filled only with loyalty and love for his commander, and yet he ended by

[1] The battle took place in 575 B.C. See *Tso chuan*, Duke Ch'eng, 16th yr.

killing him. This is what it means to practice petty loyalty and thereby betray a larger loyalty.

2. What do I mean by fixing your eyes on petty gain? Long ago Duke Hsien of Chin wanted to secure passage through the state of Yü in order to launch an attack on the state of Kuo.[2] Hsün Hsi said to the duke, "Your lordship should bribe the duke of Yü with the jade of Ch'ui-chi and the team of four horses from Ch'ü. Then if we ask for passage, he will surely grant it to us."

But the duke said, "The jade of Ch'ui-chi was a treasure of my father, the late ruler, and the team from Ch'ü are my best horses! What will I do if the duke of Yü accepts the gifts but refuses to grant us passage?"

"If he does not intend to grant us passage, he will not accept them," said Hsün Hsi. "And if he accepts them in return for passage, then it will only be as though we were removing the jade from the inner treasury and depositing it in one in the outlying districts, or transferring the horses from the palace stables to the country ones. You need not worry."

"Very well," said the duke, and sent Hsün Hsi with the jade of Ch'ui-chi and the team from Ch'ü to bribe the duke of Yü for passage. The duke of Yü, greedy for the jade and horses, was about to give his consent, when Kung Chih-ch'i admonished him, saying, "It will not do to consent! Kuo is to Yü as the jowls to the jawbone. The jowls depend on the jawbone and the jawbone depends on the jowls, and Yü and Kuo stand in the same relationship. If you grant him passage, then Kuo will be destroyed in the morning and Yü will follow it at eventide. It will not do! I beg you not to consent!"

But the duke of Yü refused to listen to him and granted

---

[2] The earlier events of the story took place in 658 B.C., the latter ones in 655 B.C. *Tso chuan*, Duke Hsi, 2d and 5th yrs.

passage to Chin. Hsün Hsi attacked and conquered [3] Kuo, and three years after the expedition he once more called up the troops and attacked and conquered Yü as well. He then brought the horses and the jade back to Duke Hsien. The duke was pleased and remarked, "The jade is as good as ever, and the teeth of the horses are even longer than before."

How did it happen that the duke of Yü saw his troops overwhelmed and his domain stripped away? Because he longed for petty profit and took no thought for the harm involved. Therefore I say: By fixing your eyes on a petty gain, you may deprive yourself of a much larger one.

3. What do I mean by behaving in a base manner? Long ago King Ling of Ch'u summoned the other feudal lords to a conference at Shen.[4] But because the crown prince of Sung arrived late, he seized him and held him prisoner, and he also insulted the ruler of Hsü and incarcerated Ch'ing Feng of Ch'i. One of his palace guards remonstrated with him, saying, "When you meet with the other feudal lords, it is unthinkable to behave with such discourtesy! This is a matter of life or death to the state. In ancient times Chieh held a meeting at Yu-jung, and the people of Yu-min revolted; Chou held a hunting conference at Li Hill and the Jung and Ti rebelled. This happened because they behaved without courtesy. I beg you to consider this!"

But the king refused to listen and went ahead doing as he pleased. Before ten years had passed [5] King Ling went on a tour of the south, and his officials took advantage of his absence to steal the throne from him. He was reduced to starva-

[3] The words "and conquered" have dropped out of the text.
[4] In 538 B.C. *Tso chuan,* Duke Chao, 4th yr.
[5] The text says "before a year had passed," but it must be faulty, since King Ling died in 529 B.C.

tion and died in Dry Valley. Hence I say: To behave in a base and willful manner and show no courtesy to the other feudal lords is the way to bring about your downfall.

4. What do I mean by longing for the sound of music? Long ago, Duke Ling [r. 534–493 B.C.] of Wei was on his way to the state of Chin, and when he reached the banks of the P'u River, he unhitched his carriages, turned his horses loose to graze, and set up camp for the night. In the middle of the night he heard someone playing a strange piece of music that pleased him greatly, but when he sent a man to question his attendants about it, they all replied that they heard nothing. He summoned his music master Chüan and said, "Someone is playing a strange piece of music, but when I sent to ask my attendants, they all replied they could hear nothing. It would almost appear to be the work of some ghost or spirit! I want you to listen for me and see if you can copy it."

"As you say," replied Master Chüan, and he sat down quietly and began to strum the lute in imitation of the music.

The next morning, Master Chüan reported to the duke. "I have the tune all right, but I have not yet had time to practice it. May I ask that we stay another night so I can do so?" "As you wish," said the duke, and they accordingly camped there another night. By the following day Master Chüan had mastered the music and they proceeded on their way to Chin.

Duke P'ing [r. 557–532] of Chin entertained them with a banquet on the Shih-i Terrace, and when the drinking was at its height, Duke Ling rose from his seat and said, "There is a new piece of music which I would like to present to you." "Excellent!" said Duke P'ing. Duke Ling then summoned Master Chüan, and instructed him to sit down beside Master K'uang, the music master of Chin, take up the lute, and play the new piece. But before he had finished Master K'uang put his hand on the lute and stopped him, saying, "This is the music of a doomed nation! You must not go on!"

"Where did this music come from?" asked Duke P'ing, and Master K'uang replied, "It was written by the music master Yen, one of the wild and licentious pieces he composed for King Chou of the Yin dynasty. When King Wu attacked King Chou, Master Yen fled to the east, and when he reached the P'u River, he threw himself into it. Hence anyone who heard this music must have done so on the banks of the P'u. He who dares to listen to this music will have his domain taken from him! You must not go on to the end!"

But Duke P'ing said, "Music is my greatest delight. Let him continue to the end!" Master Chüan accordingly continued playing to the end of the piece. Duke P'ing then turned to Master K'uang and asked, "What mode is this piece in?" "It is in the pure *shang* mode," said Master K'uang. "Is this the saddest of all the modes?" asked the duke. "It cannot compare to the pure *chih* mode," replied Master K'uang.

"May I hear something in the pure *chih* mode?" asked the duke, but Master K'uang replied, "That is impossible! Those in ancient times who listened to the pure *chih* mode were all rulers of virtue and righteousness, but you, my lord, are still deficient in virtue. You are not worthy to hear it."

"Music is the only thing I delight in," said Duke P'ing. "I beg you to let me hear a sample of it!" Master K'uang, unable to refuse, took up the lute and began to play. As he played through the first section of the music, twice times eight black cranes appeared from the south and gathered on the ridgepole of the gallery gate. As he played through the second section, they arranged themselves in a file. As he played through the third section, they stretched their necks and began to cry, beating their wings and dancing; their voices matched the music of the *kung* and *shang* modes and the sound of their singing reached to the heavens. Duke P'ing was overjoyed, and all who sat with him were filled with delight.

The duke seized a wine cup and, rising to his feet, proposed a toast to Master K'uang's happiness and long life. Then he returned to his seat and asked, "Is there no mode that is sadder than the pure *chih*?" "The pure *chüeh* is even sadder," replied Master K'uang. "May I hear something in the pure *chüeh*?" asked the duke, but Master K'uang answered, "That is impossible! In ancient times, the Yellow Emperor called the spirits together on the top of Mount T'ai. Riding in an ivory carriage drawn by six dragons, the god Pi-fang keeping pace with the linchpin, the god Ch'ih-yu stationed before him, the Wind Earl to sweep the way, the Rain Master to sprinkle the road, tigers and wolves in the vanguard, ghosts and spirits behind, writhing serpents on the ground below, phoenixes soaring above him, he called the spirits to a great assembly and created the music of the pure *chüeh* mode. But you, my lord, are still deficient in virtue. You are not worthy to hear it. If you were to hear it, I fear some misfortune would come about!"

But Duke P'ing replied, "I am an old man, and the only thing I long for is music. I beg you to let me hear it anyway!" Master K'uang, unable to refuse, began to play. As he played the first section of the music, black clouds began to rise from the northwest. With the second section, a fierce wind came forth, followed by violent rain, that tore the curtains and hangings on the terrace, overturned the cups and bowls, and shook down the tiles from the gallery roof. Those who had been sitting in the company fled in all directions, while the duke, overcome with terror, cowered in a corner of the gallery.

The state of Chin was visited by a great drought that seared the land for three years, and sores broke out all over Duke P'ing's body. Hence I say: To give no ear to government affairs but to long ceaselessly for the sound of music is the way to plunge yourself into distress.

5. What do I mean by greed and perversity? Long ago Chih Po Yao [d. 453 B.C.] led the troops of Chao, Han, and Wei in an attack on the Fan and Chung-hang families and wiped them out. After returning to his territory, he disbanded his troops for a few years, and then sent one of his men to request territory from the state of Han. Viscount K'ang of Han wished to refuse the request, but Tuan Kuei admonished him, saying, "It will not do to withold the territory! Chih Po is the kind of man who cares only for gain, and he is arrogant and perverse. If he comes to us with a demand for territory and we refuse to grant it, he will be sure to send troops against us. I hope, therefore, you will give him what he wants. If so, he will become accustomed to getting his way, and will make similar demands for land from the other states. Some of them will surely refuse him, and when they do so, he will be bound to send troops against them. In this way we can escape danger ourselves, and sit back to wait for some change in the situation!" "You are right," said Viscount K'ang, and ordered his envoy to present Chih Po with a district of ten thousand households.

Chih Po, much pleased, proceeded to send his men to the state of Wei to demand territory. Viscount Hsüan of Wei wished to refuse, but Chao Chia admonished him, saying, "He requested territory from Han, and Han gave it to him. Now he has come to us with the same request. If we refuse him, it will appear that we believe our state to be so strong internally that we are willing to incur the anger of Chih Po abroad. For should we refuse him, he will certainly send his troops against us. It would be best, therefore, to grant him the territory." "As you say," said Viscount Hsüan, and he ordered one of his men to turn over to Chih Po a district of ten thousand households.

Chih Po then sent a man to the state of Chao to demand the territories of Ts'ai and Kao-lang. Viscount Hsiang of Chao refused to give them to him, and Chih Po accordingly made a secret alliance with Han and Wei to launch an attack on Chao. Viscount Hsiang summoned Chang Meng-t'an and explained the situation to him, saying, "Chih Po is by nature friendly[6] on the surface but secretly cold and distant. Three times he has exchanged envoys with Han and Wei, and yet I have not been included in the discussions. It is certain that he is about to dispatch troops against me. Where would be a safe place for me now to take up residence?"

Chang Meng-t'an replied, "Tung Kuan-yü, who was one of the ablest ministers of your father, Lord Chien, governed the city of Chin-yang, and later Yin To took over and followed his ways, so that the influence of their good work still remains there. I would urge you to consider no other place but Chin-yang." "Very well," said the viscount, and summoned Yen-ling Sheng, ordering him to lead the army carriages and cavalry ahead to Chin-yang, and he himself followed later.

When he reached Chin-yang he inspected the inner and outer walls and the storehouses of the five government bureaus, and found the walls in poor repair, the granaries empty of provisions, the treasuries bare of money, the arsenals unstocked with weapons, and the city completely lacking in defense preparations. Much alarmed, he summoned Chang

[6] Reading *ch'in* instead of *kuei*.

Meng-t'an and said, "I have inspected the walls and store-houses of the five bureaus, and I find them completely un-prepared and unstocked. How am I to hold off an enemy?"

"I have heard," replied Chang Meng-t'an, "that when a sage governs he stores wealth among the people,[7] not in granaries and treasuries, and he works to train the people in their duty, not to repair walls and battlements. I suggest that you issue an order instructing the people to lay aside three years' supply of food and, if they have any grain left over, to bring it to the granaries. Instruct them also to lay aside funds for three years and, if they have any money left over, to bring it to the treasuries. Finally, if there are any men who are un-occupied, have them put to work repairing the walls."

The viscount issued the order that evening, and by the following day the granaries could not hold all the grain that was brought to them, there was no place left in the treasuries to store the money, and the arsenals overflowed with weapons. By the time five days had passed, the walls were in perfect repair and full provisions had been made for the defense of the city.

The viscount summoned Chang Meng-t'an again, "The walls of my city are now in good repair and provisions have been made for its defense. I have sufficient money and grain, and more weapons than I need. But what will I do for ar-rows?"

Chang Meng-t'an replied, "I have heard that when Master Tung governed Chin-yang he had the fences of all the public buildings planted with rows of cane and thorn bushes, some of which have grown very tall by now. You could cut them and use them." The viscount accordingly had some of them

---

[7] Reading *min* instead of *ch'en*.

cut and tried out, and he found them of a hardness that could not be surpassed even by the stoutest *chün-lu* bamboo.

"I have enough arrows now," said the viscount, "but what will I do for metal?" Chang Meng-t'an replied, "I have heard that when Master Tung governed Chin-yang he had the pillars and bases in the main halls of the public buildings and lodges made out of refined copper. You could remove them and use them." The viscount accordingly had the pillars and bases removed, and in this way got more metal than he needed.

When the viscount had finished issuing his war orders and had made all preparations for defense, the armies of the three other states did in fact appear. As soon as they arrived, they fell upon the walls of Chin-yang but, though they pressed the attack for three months, they were unable to take the city. They then fanned out and surrounded the city, and diverted water from the river outside Chin-yang to inundate it. Thus they besieged Chin-yang for three years. The people in the city were obliged to live in nestlike perches up above the water, and to hang their kettles from scaffoldings in order to cook. The supplies of food and provisions were almost exhausted, and even the court nobles were starving and sickly.

Viscount Hsiang said to Chang Meng-t'an, "Our provisions are gone, our strength and resources are exhausted, the officials are starving and ill, and I fear we can hold out no longer. I am going to surrender the city, but to which of the three states should I surrender?"

"They say," replied Chang Meng-t'an, "that unless wisdom can save the perishing and restore safety to the imperilled, then it is not worth honoring. I beg you to forget this plan of yours and let me try to steal out of the city in secret and visit the rulers of Han and Wei."

When Chang Meng-t'an visited the rulers of Han and Wei, he said to them, "The saying has it that when the lips are gone the teeth are cold. Now Chih Po has persuaded you two lords to join him in this attack on Chao, and Chao is about to fall. But when Chao has perished, then it will be your turn!"

"We are quite aware of that," they replied. "But Chih Po is by nature suspicious at heart and cares little for others. If we plot against him and we are discovered, then disaster is certain to fall on us. What can we do?"

"The plot comes out of your mouth, goes into my ears, and that is all," said Chang Meng-t'an. "No one else will know of it." Accordingly, the two rulers promised to join with Chao so that all three armies could turn against Chih Po, and they fixed the day for carrying out the plot. The same night they sent Chang Meng-t'an back to Chin-yang to report the prom-ise of their defection to Viscount Hsiang. On his return, the viscount greeted Chang Meng-t'an with repeated bows, his expression a mixture of joy and apprehension.

Meanwhile the rulers of Han and Wei, having dispatched Chang Meng-t'an with their promise, went the following morning to pay their customary respects to Chih Po, and as they emerged from the gate formed by his lines of war chariots, they chanced to meet his minister, Chih Kuo. Chih Kuo, after eying their faces suspiciously, went in to see Chih Po. "From the appearance of those two men, it looks as though they are going to turn against you," he said. "What was their appear-ance like?" asked Chih Po. "Their stride was arrogant and their manner haughty, with none of the restraint they have shown at other times. You had better move before they have a chance to do so."

But Chih Po replied, "I have made a solemn promise with

them that, once we have defeated Chao, we will divide its territory three ways. Since I have been this good to them, they would surely not attack or deceive me. Our troops have invested Chin-yang for three years. Now when the city is ready to fall at any moment and we are about to enjoy the spoils, what reason would they have for changing their minds? You are surely mistaken. Put it out of your mind, don't worry, and say nothing more of this!"

The following morning, when the two lords had paid their respects to Chih Po and left, they once more met Chih Kuo at the gate of the war chariots. When Chih Kuo went in to see Chih Po, he asked, "Did you tell those two men what I said to you yesterday?" "How did you guess?" said Chih Po. "This morning I met the two of them as they were on their way from visiting you," said Chih Kuo. "As soon as they saw me their faces changed and they stared hard at me. They are certain to revolt now. You had better kill them!" But Chih Po replied, "Leave the matter alone and say nothing more about it!" "That will not do!" insisted Chih Kuo. "You must kill them. Or else, if you can't bring yourself to kill them, then you must do something to win their friendship."

"And how should I win their friendship?" asked Chih Po. Chih Kuo replied, "The lord of Wei has a minister named Chao Chia whom he consults in matters of policy, and the lord of Han has a similar minister named Tuan Kuei. Both these men have the power to talk their lords into changing their plans. You should make a promise to the lords of these two ministers that, once Chao has been defeated, you will enfeoff each of them with a district of ten thousand households. If you do this, then the two rulers will think no more of turning against you."

But Chih Po replied, "I have already promised to divide

the territory of Chao three ways once it has been defeated. Now if I also have to enfeoff each of these two ministers with a district of ten thousand households, my share will be less than a third of the spoils! That won't do!"

Chih Kuo, seeing that his advice was not going to be heeded, left, and also took the precaution of changing his family name to Fu. When the evening of the day appointed for the execution of the plot came, the men of Chao killed the guards who were patrolling the river dikes and broke open a passage so that the water would inundate Chih Po's army. In their efforts to stop the water, Chih Po's men were thrown into confusion, and Han and Wei fell upon them from either side, while Viscount Hsiang of Chao led his soldiers in a frontal attack. Together they inflicted a severe defeat on Chih Po's army and took Chih Po prisoner.

Thus Chih Po was killed, his army defeated, his territory divided into three parts, and he became the laughing stock of the world. So I say: To be greedy, perverse, and too fond of profit opens the way to the destruction of the state and your own demise.

6. What do I mean by becoming infatuated with women musicians? Long ago, the king of the Jung barbarians sent Yu Yü on a state visit to Ch'in. Duke Mu [r. 659–621 B.C.] of Ch'in questioned him, saying, "I have heard general discussions of the Way, but I have never come face to face with any concrete description of it. May I ask you what was the constant principle by which the enlightened rulers of ancient times won or lost their states?"

"I have heard it said," replied Yu Yü, "that they always won their states by thrift and lost them through extravagance."

"I have not considered it beneath my dignity to ask you

about the Way," said Duke Mu. "Now why do you give me an answer like 'thrift'?"

Yu Yü replied, "I have heard it said that in ancient times, when Yao ruled the world, he ate his food from an earthen bowl and drank from an earthen pitcher, and yet within his territory, which extended as far as Chiao-chih in the south, Yu-tu in the north, and east and west to the places where the sun and moon rise and set, there was no one who did not acknowledge his sovereignty. Yao then relinquished the empire and it passed to Shun of Yü, who had new dishes made. He had wood cut in the hills and fashioned into vessels and then, after the traces of the ax and saw had been smoothed away and the surfaces had been painted with black lacquer, he had them brought to the palace to use for his tableware. But the other feudal lords considered that he was becoming extravagant, and thirteen states refused any longer to pay him allegiance.

"Later Shun ceded the empire and passed it to Yü, who had sacrificial vessels made that were varnished black on the outside and painted vermilion inside. He had cushions of woven fabric, mats of water grass with decorated edges, embellished cups and flagons, and ornamented casks and platters. Having become increasingly extravagant in his ways, he found that thirty-three of the states refused to serve him.

"The Hsia dynasty founded by Yü in time passed away and was replaced by the men of Yin, who built the great carriage of state and decorated it with nine banners. They had dishes that were carved and polished, inlaid drinking vessels, whitewashed [8] walls and plastered porches, cushions and mats that were ornamented with designs. Having become

---

[8] Reading *pai* instead of *ssu*.

even more extravagant than their predecessors, they found that fifty-three states would not obey them. The more attention the rulers paid to refinement and elegance, the fewer were those who wished to submit to them. Therefore I say that thrift is the essence of the Way."

After Yu Yü had left the room, the duke summoned his internal secretary Liao and reported what had passed. "I have heard," he said, "that the presence of a sage in a neighboring country poses a threat to all the rival states around. It is obvious that Yu Yü is a sage, and I am worried about it. What should I do?"

The internal secretary Liao replied, "They say that the king of the Jung lives in a remote and out-of-the-way region, and has never heard the music of the Middle Kingdom. You might send him some women musicians to throw his rule into disorder, and at the same time request that Yu Yü's return be postponed so that he will be deprived of Yu Yü's good advice. In that way Yu Yü and his sovereign will become estranged, and we can then lay plans to exploit the situation."

"Very good," said the duke, and ordered the internal secretary Liao to send twice times eight women musicians to the king of the Jung, and at the same time to request that Yu Yü's return be postponed.

The king of the Jung granted the request, and was so delighted with the women musicians that he ordered wine brought and banquets prepared, and spent every day listening to their music. A year passed and still he had not moved to new pastures, so that half his cattle and horses died. When Yu Yü returned, he remonstrated with the king, but the king refused to heed him, until Yu Yü finally left the state and went back to Ch'in. Duke Mu of Ch'in greeted him, honored him with the post of prime minister, and questioned him on the military strength and topography of the land of the Jung. Having obtained the information he needed, he then called out his troops and attacked the Jung, annexing twelve states and extending his domain a thousand *li*.[9] Hence I say: To become infatuated with women musicians and disregard affairs of state invites the disaster of national destruction.

7. What do I mean by leaving the palace for distant travels? Long ago Viscount T'ien Ch'eng[10] was traveling by the sea and enjoying himself so much that he issued an order to his ministers saying, "Whoever mentions going home will be put to death!"

Yen Cho-chü said to him, "My lord, you are enjoying your journey by the sea, but what if your ministers at home should be plotting against the state? Should you lose your state, how could you ever enjoy this pleasure again?"

"I have given an order that anyone who mentions going home will be put to death! You have just violated my order!" said the viscount, seizing a lance and preparing to strike Yen Cho-chü.

"In ancient times, the tyrant Chieh killed his minister Kuan Lung-feng, and Chou killed Prince Pi Kan. So you have a perfect right to kill me and make me the third victim.

[9] According to *Shih chi* 5, this took place in 623 B.C.

[10] Ch'eng is his posthumous title; his name was T'ien Ch'ang. A member of an extremely powerful ministerial family of the state of Ch'i, he succeeded his father as viscount in 485 B.C. and assured himself a place in history by murdering Duke Chien of Ch'i in 481 B.C. and placing the duke's younger brother on the throne. (See above, p. 31, n. 1.) The T'ien family eventually usurped the throne of Ch'i. In other versions of this anecdote the wandering ruler is not T'ien Ch'ang but Duke Ching (r. 547–490 B.C.) of Ch'i.

You may be sure that, like the others, I speak for the sake of the state, not for myself!" Then he stretched forth his neck and said. "Strike, my lord!"

The viscount threw down the lance, hastened to call his carriages, and returned home. Three days after he arrived he learned that some of his subjects had been plotting to prevent him from entering the capital. It was thus due to the efforts of Yen Cho-chü that Viscount T'ien Ch'eng was finally able to seize control of the state of Ch'i. Hence I say: To leave the palace for distant travels leads to grave peril for yourself.

8. What do I mean by failing to heed your loyal ministers when you are at fault? Long ago Duke Huan of Ch'i nine times summoned the other feudal lords to conference, brought unity and peace to the empire, and became the first of the five dictators, and Kuan Chung [d. 645 B.C.] aided him. When Kuan Chung grew old and could no longer serve the duke, he retired to his home to rest. Duke Huan called upon him there, and said, "Father Chung, you are ill and living in retirement. If by some unlucky chance you should not rise again from your sickbed, to whom can I entrust the affairs of state?"

"I am an old man and cannot answer such a question," said Kuan Chung. "They say that no one knows the ministers better than their sovereign, and no one knows the sons better than their father. You should try to make the decision for yourself."

"How would Pao Shu-ya do?" asked the duke, but Kuan Chung replied, "Impossible! Pao Shu-ya is by nature stubborn, perverse, and given to displays of arrogance. Being stubborn, he will offend the people with his unruly ways; being perverse, he will never win their hearts; and being

arrogant, he will never secure the cooperation of his subordinates. And with all these faults, he has not the sense to be
fearful. He cannot act as aid to a dictator."

"Then what about Shu-tiao?" asked the duke, but Kuan
Chung replied, "Impossible! It is only human nature to look
out for one's own body. Yet Shu-tiao, knowing that you are
jealous and dote on your ladies in waiting, castrated himself
so that he could be put in charge of the harem. If he cares
so little for himself, how can he care for you?"

"Then what about Prince K'ai-fang of Wei?" asked the
duke, but Kuan Chung replied, "He will never do. The states
of Wei and Ch'i are no more than ten days' journey apart
and yet, since K'ai-fang came to your court, he has been so
intent upon ingratiating himself with you that he has not
been home to see his father or mother in fifteen years! This
is contrary to human nature. If he has no affection for his own
parents, how can he have any affection for you?"

"What about Yi-ya?" asked the duke, but Kuan Chung
replied, "He will not do. He was in charge of supplying your
table with delicacies and, knowing that the only thing you
had never tasted was human flesh, he steamed the head of his
own son and presented it to you. You know this as well as I.
There is no one who does not feel affection for his son, and
yet here is a man who would cook his own son and present
him on a tray to his ruler. If he does not love his son, how
can he love you?"

"In that case, who will do?" asked the duke. "Hsi P'eng,"
said Kuan Chung. "By nature he is steadfast of heart and
honest with others, few in his desires and full of good faith.
Being steadfast of heart, he can serve as a model; being honest
with others, he can be entrusted with important undertakings;
being few in desires, he can be trusted to oversee the masses;

and being full of good faith, he can establish friendly relations with neighboring states. He can act as aid to a dictator. I hope you will employ him."

"As you say," said the duke. But a year or so later, when Kuan Chung died, the duke did not employ Hsi P'eng, but turned matters over to Shu-tiao instead. After Shu-tiao had had charge of affairs of state for three years, Duke Huan journeyed south on a pleasure trip to T'ang-fu. Shu-tiao then led Yi-ya, Prince K'ai-fang of Wei, and the other high ministers in a revolt. Duke Huan died of thirst and hunger in guarded confinement in a chamber of the South Gate Palace, and his body remained unburied for three months until the maggots began to crawl out of the chamber door.

Why was it that, though his armies marched across the empire at will and he himself was the first of the five dictators, Duke Huan was in the end assassinated by his ministers, lost his fair reputation, and became the laughing stock of the world? It was because of his failure to heed Kuan Chung. Hence I say: To fail to heed your loyal ministers when you are at fault, but to insist upon having your own way, will in time destroy your good reputation and make you the laughing stock of others.

9. What do I mean by taking no account of internal strength [but relying solely upon your allies abroad]? In former times Ch'in launched an attack on the city of Yi-yang, and the men of the Han clan, who held possession of Yi-yang, were sorely pressed.[11] Kung-chung P'eng said to the ruler of Han, "Our allies cannot be relied upon to help us. It would be best to ask Chang Yi to arrange peace terms for

[11] According to *Shih chi* 15 and 45, the attack on Yi-yang took place in 307–306 B.C. But the *Shih chi* relates the rest of the anecdote to an earlier attack made by Ch'in on Han in 316–314 B.C.

us with Ch'in. We could bribe Ch'in by presenting it with one of our larger cities, and then join Ch'in in an attack on Ch'u to the south. In this way we can solve our difficulties with Ch'in and shift the harm to Ch'u." "Excellent!" said the ruler of Han, and he ordered Kung-chung P'eng to make preparations to journey west and negotiate peace with Ch'in.

When the king of Ch'u heard of this he was terrified and summoned Ch'en Chen and informed him of the situation. "Kung-chung P'eng of Han is about to go west to negotiate peace with Ch'in. What shall we do?" he asked. "Ch'in, having gotten a city from Han, will call out its best troops and join with Han in facing south to march against Ch'u," said Ch'en Chen. "The king of Ch'in has long prayed in the temple of his ancestors for an opportunity like this! Ch'u is bound to suffer. I beg you to despatch an envoy at once to the court of Han, accompanied by many carriages and bearing lavish gifts, to say to the Han ruler, 'Small as our unworthy state is, we have called out all our troops, and we trust you will remain firm in your defiance of Ch'in. We accordingly ask that you send an envoy to enter our borders and observe the forces which we have mobilized to aid you.'"

When this plan had been carried out Han did in fact send a man to Ch'u. The king of Ch'u accordingly called out his chariots and horsemen and ranged them along the road leading north to Han. He then said to the Han envoy, "You may report to the ruler of Han that the troops of my unworthy state are just about to cross the border."

When the envoy returned with this message the ruler of Han was greatly pleased and ordered Kung-chung P'eng to cease preparations for the journey to Ch'in. But Kung-chung P'eng said, "That will not do! Ch'in is actually afflicting[12] us,

---

[12] Reading *k'u* instead of *kan.*

whereas Ch'u has only *said that* it will come to our rescue.
If we heed the empty words of Ch'u and make light of the
real danger that the powerful forces of Ch'in are posing, we
will place the state in grave peril!"

The ruler of Han, however, refused to listen to him and
Kung-chung P'eng in great anger returned to his home and
for ten days did not appear at court. Meanwhile the siege
of Yi-yang became more and more critical. The ruler of Han
despatched envoys urging Ch'u to send its reinforcements,
but though the envoys followed so close upon each other's
heels that their caps and carriage covers were within sight
on the road, no troops ever arrived. Yi-yang finally capitulated,
and the ruler of Han became the laughing stock of the other
feudal lords. Hence I say: To take no account of internal
strength but rely solely upon your allies abroad will place the
state in grave danger of dismemberment.

10. What do I mean by ignoring the demands of courtesy,
though your state is small? Long ago, when Prince Ch'ung-
erh of Chin fled from his home, he visited the state of
Ts'ao.[13] The ruler of Ts'ao made him strip to the waist and
stared at him,[14] while Hsi Fu-chi and Shu Chan waited in
attendance. Later Shu Chan said to the ruler of Ts'ao, "I can
see that the prince of Chin is no ordinary man, and yet you
have treated him with discourtesy. If he should sometime
return to his state and call out its troops, I fear that harm
would come to Ts'ao. It would be best for you to kill him

[13] Prince Ch'ung-erh, the son of Duke Hsien of Chin, was forced to flee
from Chin in 656 B.C. because of the machinations of his evil stepmother,
Lady Li. The *Tso chuan* records his visit to Ts'ao under the year 637 B.C.
(Duke Hsi, 23d yr.).

[14] Ch'ung-erh was said to have had peculiar ribs that grew together, and
the ruler of Ts'ao was anxious to see them for himself. According to the
version of the story in the *Tso chuan*, he peeked in while the prince was
taking a bath.

now." But the ruler of Ts'ao did not heed this advice.

Hsi Fu-chi returned home, deeply disturbed. His wife asked him, "Why do you come home with such an unhappy look on your face?" Hsi Fu-chi replied, "They say that good luck benefits one person alone, but bad luck spreads to others. Today our lord summoned the prince of Chin and treated him discourteously. I was attending him at the time, and therefore I am disturbed."

"I have seen the prince of Chin," said his wife. "He is fit to be the ruler of a state of ten thousand chariots, and his followers are fit to be the ministers of such a state. Now he is hard pressed, and in his wanderings in exile has come to visit Ts'ao, and yet Ts'ao has treated him discourteously. If he ever returns to his own state, he will surely punish these insults, and Ts'ao will be the first to suffer. Why don't you do something now to show him that you do not regard him in the same way as the ruler of Ts'ao does?"

"You are right," said Hsi Fu-chi. He then filled several pots with gold, covered the gold with gifts of food, and placed pieces of jade on top, sending someone at night to present them to the prince. When the prince received the messenger, he bowed twice, accepted the food, but returned the pieces of jade.

From Ts'ao the prince proceeded to Ch'u, and then to Ch'in. Three years after he had gone to Ch'in, Duke Mu of Ch'in summoned his ministers to conference and announced, "In the past, as all the feudal lords know, Duke Hsien of Chin was a close friend of mine. Now it has been some ten years since death unkindly took him away from his ministers. His heir is not a good man, and I fear that if things continue in this way he may bring difilement to the temple of his ancestors and deprive the state's altars of the soil and grain of their constant sacrifices. If I were to make no effort to restore stability in the state, I would be neglecting my duty as a friend of Duke Hsien. I would therefore like to assist Ch'ung-erh and install him on the throne of Chin. What is your opinion?" The ministers all replied, "Excellent!" and Duke Mu accordingly called out his troops, and assigned five hundred leather covered war chariots, two thousand picked horsemen, and fifty thousand foot soldiers to assist Ch'ung-erh in entering the capital of Chin. Thus he set up Ch'ung-erh as ruler of Chin.

Three years after he became ruler Ch'ung-erh called out his troops and attacked Ts'ao.[15] At the same time he sent men to announce to the ruler of Ts'ao, "You must lower Shu Chan from the city walls and hand him over to me, for I intend to kill him in punishment for his behavior!" He also sent men to announce to Hsi Fu-chi, "My troops are besieging the city. I know that you will not desert your sovereign, but I want you to mark the gates of your compound. I will issue an order to my troops instructing them not to trespass on it." When the people of Ts'ao heard of this they brought their parents and relatives and over seven hundred families took refuge in the residential quarter of Hsi Fu-chi. Such is the reward of courtesy.

Ts'ao was a small state pressed between Chin and Ch'u, and the safety of its ruler was as precarious as a pile of eggs, and yet he conducted his affairs without courtesy. This is the reason his line came to an end. Hence I say: To ignore the demands of courtesy, though your state is small, and to fail to learn from the remonstrances of your ministers, are acts that lead to the downfall of your line.

[15] According to the *Spring and Autumn Annals* (Duke Hsi, 28th yr.), the attack took place in 632 B.C.

THE DIFFICULTIES OF PERSUASION[1]

(SECTION 12)

On the whole, the difficult thing about persuading others is not that one lacks the knowledge needed to state his case nor the audacity to exercise his abilities to the full. On the whole, the difficult thing about persuasion is to know the mind of the person one is trying to persuade and to be able to fit one's words to it.

If the person you are trying to persuade is out to establish a reputation for virtue, and you talk to him about making a fat profit, then he will regard you as low-bred, accord you a shabby and contemptuous reception, and undoubtedly send you packing. If the person you are trying to persuade is on the contrary interested in a fat profit, and you talk to him about a virtuous reputation, he will regard you as witless and out of touch with reality, and will never heed your arguments. If the person you are trying to persuade is secretly out for big gain but ostensibly claims to be interested in a virtuous name alone, and you talk to him about a reputation for virtue, then he will pretend to welcome and heed you, but in fact will shunt you aside; if you talk to him about making a big gain, he will secretly follow your advice but ostensibly reject you. These are facts that you must not fail to consider carefully.

Undertakings succeed through secrecy but fail through

---

[1] This chapter, with frequent textual differences, is recorded in *Shih chi* 63, the biography of Han Fei Tzu.

being found out. Though the ruler himself has not yet divulged his plans, if you in your discussions happen to hit upon his hidden motives, then you will be in danger. If the ruler is ostensibly seeking one thing but actually is attempting to accomplish something quite different, and you perceive not only his ostensible objective but the real motives behind his actions as well, then you will likewise be in danger. If you happen to think up some unusual scheme for the ruler which meets with his approval, and some other person of intelligence manages by outside means to guess what it is and divulges the secret to the world, then the ruler will suppose that it was you who gave it away and you will be in danger. If you have not yet won substantial reward and favor and yet your words are extremely apt and wise, then if the ruler heeds them and the undertaking is successful, he will forget to reward you; and if he does not heed them and the undertaking fails, he will regard you with suspicion and you will be in danger. If some person of eminence takes a brief step in the wrong direction and you immediately launch into a lecture on ritual principles and challenge his misdeed, then you will be in danger. If some eminent person gets hold of a good scheme somewhere and plans to use it to win merit for himself, and you happen to know where he got it, then you will be in danger. If you try forcibly to talk a person into doing what he cannot do, or stopping what he cannot stop, then you will be in danger.

If you talk to the ruler about men of real worth, he will think you are implying that he is no match for them; if you talk to him of petty men, he will think you are attempting to use your influence to get your friends into office; if you talk to him about what he likes, he will suspect you of trying to utilize him; if you talk about what he hates, he will suspect you of trying to test his patience. If you speak too bluntly and to the point, he will consider you unlearned and will shun you; if you speak too eloquently and in too great detail, he will consider you pretentious and will reject[2] you. If you are too sketchy in outlining your ideas, he will think you a coward who is too fainthearted to say what he really means; if you are too exuberant and long-winded in stating your proposals, he will think you an uncouth bumpkin who is trying to talk down to him. These are the difficulties of persuasion; you cannot afford to be ignorant of them!

The important thing in persuasion is to learn how to play up the aspects that the person you are talking to is proud of, and play down the aspects he is ashamed of. Thus, if the person has some urgent personal desire, you should show him that it is his public duty to carry it out and urge him not to delay. If he has some mean objective in mind and yet cannot restrain himself, you should do your best to point out to him whatever admirable aspects it may have and to minimize the reprehensible ones. If he has some lofty objective in mind and yet does not have the ability needed to realize it, you should do your best to point out to him the faults and bad aspects of such an objective and make it seem a virtue not to pursue it. If he is anxious to make a show of wisdom and ability, mention several proposals which are different from the one you have in mind but of the same general nature in order to supply him with ideas; then let him build on your words, but pretend that you are unaware that he is doing so, and in this way abet his wisdom.

If you wish to urge a policy of peaceful coexistence, then be sure to expound it in terms of lofty ideals, but also hint that it is commensurate with the ruler's personal interests.

[2] Reading *ch'i* instead of *chiao.*

If you wish to warn the ruler against dangerous and injurious policies, then make a show of the fact that they invite reproach and moral censure, but also hint that they are inimical to his personal interests.

Praise other men whose deeds are like those of the person you are talking to; commend other actions which are based upon the same policies as his. If there is someone else who is guilty of the same vice he is, be sure to gloss it over by showing that it really does no great harm; if there is someone else who has suffered the same failure he has, be sure to defend it by demonstrating that it is not a loss after all. If he prides himself on his physical prowess, do not antagonize him by mentioning the difficulties he has encountered in the past; if he considers himself an expert at making decisions, do not anger him by pointing out his past errors; if he pictures himself a sagacious planner, do not tax him with his failures. Make sure that there is nothing in your ideas as a whole that will vex your listener, and nothing about your words that will rub him the wrong way, and then you may exercise your powers of rhetoric to the fullest. This is the way to gain the confidence and intimacy of the person you are addressing and to make sure that you are able to say all you have to say without incurring his suspicion.

Yi Yin became a cook and Po-li Hsi a captive slave, so they could gain the ear of the ruler.[3] These men were sages, and yet they could not avoid shouldering hard tasks for the sake of advancement and demeaning themselves in this way. Therefore you too should become a cook or a slave when necessary; if this enables you to gain the confidence of the

---

[3] Yi Yin became a cook in the kitchen of Ch'eng T'ang, the founder of the Shang dynasty; Po-li Hsi became a slave at the court of Duke Mu of Ch'in (r. 659–621 B.C.).

ruler and save the state, then it is no disgrace for a man of ability to take such a course.

If you are able to fulfill long years of service with the ruler, enjoy his fullest favor and confidence, lay long-range plans for him without ever arousing suspicion, and when necessary oppose him in argument without incurring blame, then you may achieve merit by making clear to him what is profitable and what is harmful, and bring glory to yourself by your forthright judgments of right and wrong. When ruler and minister aid and sustain each other in this way, persuasion may be said to have reached its fulfillment.

In ancient times Duke Wu of Cheng wanted to attack the state of Hu, and so he first married his daughter to the ruler of Hu in order to fill his mind with thoughts of pleasure. Then he told his ministers, "I want to launch a military campaign. What would be a likely state to attack?" The high official Kuan Ch'i-ssu replied, "Hu could be attacked," whereupon Duke Wu flew into a rage and had him executed,[4] saying, Hu is a brother state! What do you mean by advising me to attack it!" The ruler of Hu, hearing of this, assumed that Cheng was friendly towards him and therefore took no precautions to defend himself from Cheng. The men of Cheng then made a surprise attack on Hu and seized it.

Once there was a rich man of Sung. When the dirt wall around his house collapsed in a heavy rain, his son said, "If you don't rebuild it, thieves will surely break in," and the old man who lived next door told him the same thing. When night fell, thieves actually broke in and made off with a large share of the rich man's wealth. The rich man's family praised the son for his wisdom, but eyed the old man next door with suspicion.

---

[4] According to the *Bamboo Annals,* this took place in 763 B.C.

Both these men—the high official Kuan Ch'i-ssu and the old man next door—spoke the truth, and yet one was actually executed for his words, while the other cast suspicion on himself. It is not difficult to know a thing; what is difficult is to know how to use what you know. Jao Chao spoke the truth but, though he was regarded as a sage by the men of Chin, he was executed by those of Ch'in.[5] This is something you cannot afford not to examine.

In ancient times Mi Tzu-hsia won favor with the ruler of Wei.[6] According to the laws of the state of Wei, anyone who secretly made use of the ruler's carriage was punished by having his feet amputated. When Mi Tzu-hsia's mother fell ill, someone slipped into the palace at night to report this to Mi Tzu-hsia. Mi Tzu-hsia forged an order from the ruler, got into the ruler's carriage, and went off to see her, but when the ruler heard of it, he only praised him, saying, "How filial! For the sake of his mother he forgot all about the danger of having his feet cut off!" Another day Mi Tzu-hsia was strolling with the ruler in an orchard and, biting into a peach and finding it sweet, he stopped eating and gave the remaining half to the ruler to enjoy. "How sincere is your love for me!" exclaimed the ruler. "You forget your own appetite and think only of giving me good things to eat!" Later, however, when Mi Tzu-hsia's looks had faded and the ruler's passion for him had cooled, he was accused of committing some crime against his lord. "After all," said the ruler, "he once stole my carriage, and another time he gave me a half-eaten peach to eat!" Mi Tzu-hsia was actually acting no differently from the

---

[5] Jao Chao is mentioned briefly in the *Tso chuan,* Duke Wen, 13th year (614 B.C.), as a minister of Ch'in who saw through a plot of the men of Chin, but the exact anecdote which Han Fei Tzu is referring to here is not known.

[6] Duke Ling of Wei (r. 534–493 B.C.).

way he always had; the fact that he was praised in the early days, and accused of a crime later on, was because the ruler's love had turned to hate.

If you gain the ruler's love, your wisdom will be appreciated and you will enjoy his favor as well; but if he hates you, not only will your wisdom be rejected, but you will be regarded as a criminal and thrust aside. Hence men who wish to present their remonstrances and expound their ideas must not fail to ascertain the ruler's loves and hates before launching into their speeches.

The beast called the dragon can be tamed [7] and trained to the point where you may ride on its back. But on the underside of its throat it has scales a foot in diameter that curl back from the body, and anyone who chances to brush against them is sure to die. The ruler of men too has his bristling scales. Only if a speaker can avoid brushing against them will he have any hope for success.

[7] Reading *jao* instead of *jou*.

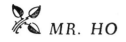 *MR. HO*

(SECTION 13)

Once a man of Ch'u named Mr. Ho, having found a piece of jade matrix in the Ch'u Mountains, took it to court and presented it to King Li.[1] King Li instructed the jeweler to examine it, and the jeweler reported, "It is only a stone." The king, supposing that Ho was trying to deceive him, ordered that his left foot be cut off in punishment. In time King Li passed away and King Wu came to the throne, and Ho once more took his matrix and presented it to King Wu. King Wu ordered his jeweler to examine it, and again the jeweler reported, "It is only a stone." The king, supposing that Ho was trying to deceive him as well, ordered that his right foot be cut off. Ho, clasping the matrix to his breast, went to the foot of the Ch'u Mountains, where he wept for three days and nights, and when all his tears were cried out, he wept blood in their place. The king, hearing of this, sent someone to question him. "Many people in the world have had their feet amputated—why do you weep so piteously over it?" the man asked. Ho replied, "I do not grieve because my feet have been cut off. I grieve because a precious jewel is dubbed a mere stone, and a man of integrity is called a deceiver. This is why I weep." The king then ordered the jeweler to cut and polish the matrix, and when he had done so a precious jewel emerged. Accordingly it was named "The Jade of Mr. Ho."

[1] The famous anecdote of Mr. Ho's jade is found in many early Chinese philosophical works. In some versions, Mr. Ho's name is given as Pien Ho. The list of Ch'u kings to whom he presented his treasure varies.

Rulers are always anxious to lay their hands on pearls and precious stones. Though Ho presented a matrix whose true beauty was not yet apparent, he certainly did no harm to the ruler thereby; and yet he had to have both feet cut off before the real nature of his treasure was finally recognized. This is how hard it is to get a treasure acknowledged. Rulers nowadays are not nearly so anxious to get hold of laws and state policies as they are to get hold of Ho's jade, and they are concerned about putting a stop to the private evils and deceptions of the officials and common people. Under these circumstances, if a man who truly understands the Way hopes to avoid punishment, his only resort is simply not to present to the ruler any uncut jewels of wisdom and statecraft.

If the ruler follows set policies, then the high ministers will be unable to make arbitrary decisions, and those who are close to him will not dare try to sell their influence. If the magistrates enforce the laws, then vagabonds will have to return to their farm work and wandering knights will be sent to the battlefield where they belong to face the dangers of their profession. In effect, then, laws and policies are actually inimical to the private interests of the officials and common people. Hence, if a ruler does not have the strength of character to defy the counsels of the high ministers, rise above the criticisms of the common people, and heed only that advice which truly accords with the Way, then the planners of law and policy may persist, like Mr. Ho, until they face the death penalty itself, and yet the true value of their words will never be acknowledged.

In former times Wu Ch'i advised King Tao [r. 401–381 B.C.] of Ch'u on the customs of the state. "The high ministers have too much power," he said, "and the enfeoffed lords are too numerous; hence they pose a threat to their ruler above, and oppress the common people under them. Such a path will only impoverish the state and debilitate its army. It would be better for you to confiscate all titles and stipends of the enfeoffed lords after the third generation, reduce[2] the ranks and salaries of your various officials, prune away the offices that serve no vital need, and employ only those men who have proved themselves able and experienced." King Tao acted on this advice, but a year later he passed away and Wu Ch'i was torn limb from limb by the men of Ch'u.

Lord Shang[3] taught Duke Hsiao [r. 361–338 B.C.] of Ch'in how to organize the people into groups of five and ten families that would spy on each other and be corporately responsible for crimes committed by their members; he advised him to burn the *Book of Odes* and *Book of Documents*[4] and elucidate the laws and regulations, to reject the private requests of powerful families and concentrate upon furthering the interests of the royal family; to forbid people to wander about in search of political office, and to glorify the lot of those who devote themselves to agriculture and warfare. Duke Hsiao put his suggestions into practice, and as a result the position of the ruler became secure and respected, and the state grew rich and powerful. But eight years later Duke Hsiao passed away, and Lord Shang was tied to two chariots and torn apart by the men of Ch'in.

Ch'u, failing to continue the policies of Wu Ch'i, suffered

---

[2] Reading *ts'ai-chien* instead of *chüeh-mieh*.

[3] Wei Yang or Kung-sun Yang, a Legalist statesman and the reputed author of the early Legalist work, the *Book of Lord Shang*.

[4] If Han Fei Tzu's statement is in fact correct, Duke Hsiao does not seem to have carried out his piece of advice; it remained for the First Emperor of the Ch'in dynasty to institute a systematic burning of the *Odes* and *Documents*.

from foreign incursion and internal chaos; Ch'in, applying
Lord Shang's laws, became rich and powerful. Yet, though
both men spoke what was apt and true, why was it that Wu
Ch'i was torn limb from limb, and Lord Shang was pulled
apart by chariots? Because the high ministers resented their
laws and the common people hated orderly government. And
in the present age the high ministers covet power and the
common people find satisfaction in disorder to a far greater
degree than did the men of Ch'u and Ch'in in the times I have
described. If there is no King Tao or Duke Hsiao to heed
advice, then how will the planners of law and policy ever be
willing to risk the fate of Wu Ch'i and Lord Shang in order
to elucidate their laws and policies? This is why our present
age is in chaos and lacks a true dictator or king.

PRECAUTIONS WITHIN
THE PALACE

(SECTION 17)

It is hazardous for the ruler of men to trust others, for he
who trusts others will be controlled by others. Ministers have
no bonds of flesh and blood which tie them to their ruler; it
is only the force of circumstance which compels them to serve
him. Hence those who act as ministers never for a moment
cease trying to spy into their sovereign's mind, and yet the
ruler of men sits above them in indolence and pride. That is
why there are rulers in the world who face intimidation and
sovereigns who are murdered. If the ruler puts too much
trust in his son, then evil ministers will find ways to utilize
the son for the accomplishment of their private schemes. Thus
Li Tui, acting as aid to the king of Chao, starved the Father
of the Ruler to death.[1] If the ruler puts too much trust in his
consort, then evil ministers will find ways to utilize the consort for the accomplishment of their private schemes. Thus
the actor Shih aided Lady Li to bring about the death of
Shen-sheng and to set Hsi-ch'i on the throne.[2] Now if some-

[1] "Father of the Ruler" was a title assumed by King Wu-ling of Chao
when he abdicated in 291 B.C. in favor of his son, King Hui-wen. In 294
B.C. his palace was surrounded by soldiers headed by the high minister Li
Tui, and after some three months of confinement he died of starvation.
Shih chi 43.

[2] Lady Li, a later consort of Duke Hsien of Chin, succeeded, with the
aid of a court actor named Shih, in casting suspicion on the heir apparent,
Shen-sheng, and forcing him to commit suicide in 656 B.C. Her own son
by the duke, Hsi-ch'i, was then made heir apparent and succeeded to the
throne in 651 B.C. *Kuo yü, Chin yü* 2.

one as close to the ruler as his own consort, and as dear to him as his own son, still cannot be trusted, then obviously no one else is to be trusted either.

Moreover, whether one is ruler of a state of ten thousand chariots or of a thousand only, it is quite likely that his consort, his concubines, or the son he has designated as heir to his throne will wish for his early death. How do I know this is so? A wife is not bound to her husband by any ties of blood. If he loves her, she remains close to him; if not, she becomes estranged. The saying goes, "If the mother is favored, the son will be embraced." But if this is so, then the opposite must be, "If the mother is despised, the son will be cast away." A man at fifty has not yet lost interest in sex, and yet at thirty a woman's beauty has already faded. If a woman whose beauty has already faded waits upon a man still occupied by thoughts of sex, then she will be spurned and disfavored,[3] and her son will stand little chance of succeeding to the throne. This is why consorts and concubines long for the early death of the ruler.

If the consort can become queen dowager and her son ascend the throne, then any law she issues will be carried out, any prohibition she decrees will be heeded. She may enjoy the delights of sex as often as she ever did while her late lord was alive and may rule a state of ten thousand chariots in any way she pleases without fear of suspicion. This is why we have secret poisonings, stranglings, and knifings. As the *Spring and Autumn Annals of T'ao Tso*[4] says, "Less than half of all rulers die from illness." If the ruler does not understand this, then he lays himself open to revolt on all sides.

---

[3] Omitting the *ssu*, which is superfluous.
[4] This work is otherwise unknown.

Thus it is said: When those who stand to profit by the ruler's death are many, he is in peril.

The charioteer Wang Liang was good to his horses, and Kou-chien, the king of Yüeh, was good to his men, the one so that they would run for him, the other so that they would fight for him. A physician will often suck men's wounds clean and hold the bad blood in his mouth, not because he is bound to them by any tie of kinship but because he knows there is profit in it. The carriage maker making carriages hopes that men will grow rich and eminent; the carpenter fashioning coffins hopes that men will die prematurely. It is not that the carriage maker is kindhearted and the carpenter a knave. It is only that if men do not become rich and eminent, the carriages will never sell, and if men do not die, there will be no market for coffins. The carpenter has no feeling of hatred toward others; he merely stands to profit by their death. In the same way, when consorts, concubines, and heirs apparent have organized their cliques, they long for the ruler's death for, unless he dies, their position will never be really strong. They have no feeling of hatred toward the ruler; they merely stand to profit by his death. The ruler therefore must not fail to keep close watch on those who might profit by his death.

Though the sun and moon are surrounded by halos, the real danger to them comes from within.[5] Prepare as you may against those who hate you, calamity will come to you from those you love.

[5] Han Fei Tzu is probably referring to the folk tale of the toad that lives in the moon and the three-legged crow that lives in the sun, which were said to cause the eclipses of these bodies. It is not certain how much the men of Han Fei Tzu's time understood about the true nature of eclipses, but here he finds it convenient for his argument to regard them as internally caused.

Therefore the enlightened ruler does not rush into any undertaking that he has not properly studied beforehand nor does he eat any unusual foods. He listens to reports from afar and scrutinizes the men close to him in order to ascertain the faults of those within and without the palace. He examines the agreements and disagreements in debate in order to determine how the various factions in the government shape up. He compares proposals and results to make certain that words are backed up by facts. He demands that what comes after shall match what went before, governs the masses according to the law, and carefully checks on the various motives of all. If he can make certain that men do not receive any unearned rewards nor overstep their authority, that death penalties are justly handed out and no crime goes unpunished, then evil and malicious men will find no opening to carry out their private schemes.

If too much compulsory labor service is demanded of the people, they feel afflicted, and this will give rise to local power groups. When local power groups have arisen, they will begin exercising the right to exempt the people from labor service, and once they are able to do this, their leaders will grow rich on bribes. To afflict the people and thereby enrich men of influence, to create power groups and thereby relinquish your authority to your ministers are not the way to bring long lasting benefit to the world. Hence it is said, if labor services are few, the people will be content; if the people are content, there will be no opportunity for men to exercise undue authority on the lower levels and power groups will disappear. Once power groups have been wiped out, then all right to dispense favors will reside with the sovereign.

It is obvious that, under normal conditions, water will overcome fire. But if a kettle comes between them, the water will bubble and boil itself completely dry on top, while the fire goes on burning merrily away underneath, the water having been deprived of the means by which it customarily overcomes fire. It is just as obvious that government should be able to put an end to evil in the same way as water overcomes fire. But if the officials whose duty it is to uphold the law instead play the part of the kettle, then the laws will be clear only in the mind of the ruler alone, and he will have been deprived of the means by which to prohibit evil.

Judging from the tales handed down from high antiquity and the incidents recorded in the *Spring and Autumn Annals*,[6] those men who violated the laws, committed treason, and carried out major acts of evil always worked through some eminent and highly placed minister. And yet the laws and regulations are customarily designed to prevent evil among the humble and lowly people, and it is upon them alone that penalties and punishments fall. Hence the common people lose hope and are left with no place to air their grievances. Meanwhile the high ministers band together and work as one man to cloud the vision of the ruler. In order to demonstrate that they have no private schemes, they pretend on the outside to be at odds with one another, though in secret they are friendly enough, acting as ears and eyes for each other to spy out flaws in the ruler's defense. The ruler, his vision thus clouded and obstructed, has no path by which to obtain true information; though he retains the name of sovereign, he has lost the reality, and his ministers are free to enforce the laws as they please. This is what happened to the Son of Heaven

---

[6] It is not clear whether this refers to the chronicle of the state of **Lu,** supposed to have been compiled by Confucius, which bears this title, or is a generic term for the chronicles of the various feudal states.

of the Chou dynasty. If the ruler lends even a little of his power to others, then superior and inferior will change places. Hence it is said that no ministers should be allowed to borrow the power and authority of the ruler.[7]

---

[7] The text of the latter half of this paragraph is rather scrappy and disorganized, and it has been surmised that parts of it may actually be bits of commentary that have erroneously been copied into the text.

FACING SOUTH [1]

(SECTION 18)

This is where rulers go wrong: having assigned certain ministers to office, they then try to use unassigned men to check the power of the assigned. They justify this policy by claiming that the interests of the assigned and the unassigned will be mutually inimical, but in fact the rulers find themselves falling under the power of the unassigned, for the men they are trying to check today are the men whom they used in previous days to check others. If the rulers cannot make the law clear and use it to restrain the authority of the high ministers, then they will have no means to win the confidence of the people at large.

If the ruler of men discards the law, and instead attempts to use some of his ministers to control others, then those who love each other will band together in groups for mutual praise, and those who hate each other will form cliques for mutual slander. With praise and slander striving to shout each other down, the ruler will become bewildered and confused.

Those who act as ministers believe that, unless they can somehow establish a fine reputation or persuade someone to make a special plea for them, they will never advance in office; that unless they turn their backs on law and concentrate power in their own hands, they can never wield authority; and that unless they rely upon a mask of loyalty and good faith, they can never circumvent the prohibitions. Yet these

[1] I.e., being a ruler; see above, p. 24, n. 5.

three types of behavior in fact serve only to delude the sovereign and destroy the law. So the ruler of men must make certain that, no matter how wise and capable his ministers may be, they are never allowed to turn their backs on the law and concentrate power in their own hands; no matter how worthy their actions may be, they are never allowed to presume upon their achievements and snatch rewards that belong to others; no matter how loyal and trustworthy they may be, they are never allowed to discard the law and circumvent the prohibitions. This is what it means to make the law clear.

The ruler of men is sometimes misled in undertakings and blinded by words. These are two dangers which he must not fail to consider carefully.

Ministers come blithely forward with a proposal for an undertaking and, because the funds they ask for are small, the ruler is duped by the proposal; misled as to its true nature, he fails to examine it thoroughly, but instead is filled with admiration for the men who made it. In this way ministers are able to use undertakings to gain power over the ruler. This is what it means to be misled in undertakings, and he who is so misled will be beset by hazard.

If, when a minister comes forward with a proposal, he asks for meager funds but, after he has retired to put it into effect his expenditures are very large, then although the undertaking may produce results, the proposal was not made in good faith. He who speaks in bad faith is guilty of a crime and, though his undertaking has achieved results, he should receive no reward.[2] If this rule is obeyed, then the ministers will not dare to dress up their words in an effort to delude the sovereign.

---

[a] Supplying a *sui* before *yu* and reading *pu* instead of *pi*.

The way of the ruler is to make certain that, if what a minister says beforehand does not tally with what he says later, or what he says later does not tally with what he has said previously, then although he may have fulfilled his task with distinction, he is condemned to certain punishment. This is what it means to hold your subordinates responsible.

If a minister is planning to bring a proposal for some undertaking before the ruler but fears that it will meet with criticism, he will be certain to announce beforehand, "Anyone who questions this undertaking does so simply out of jealousy." The ruler, with these words firmly fixed in his mind, will pay no further heed to the advice of other ministers, while they for their part, fearful of the effect of such words, will not venture to question the undertaking. When these two circumstances prevail, then truly loyal ministers will go unheeded and only those who have managed to acquire a reputation will be put in charge. This is what it means to be blinded by words, and he who is so blinded will end up in the power of his ministers.

The way of the ruler is to make certain that ministers are called to account for the words they speak and are also called to account for the words they fail to speak. If the beginning and end of their words fail to tally, if their arguments lack proof, then they are called to account for what they have spoken. If they attempt to evade responsibility by saying nothing, although they hold important positions, then they are called to account for not speaking. The ruler of men must make certain that, when his ministers speak, he understands the beginning and end of what they say and can hold them responsible for matching it with facts; and when they fail to speak, he must inquire into the causes for their reticence and hold them responsible for that as well. If this is done, then ministers will not dare to speak out recklessly, nor will they dare to remain silent, for they will know that both speech and silence will be equally called to account.

When the ruler of men wishes to carry out some undertaking, if he does not acquire a clear understanding of all the factors involved, but simply makes obvious his desire to carry it out, then the work will bring no profit, but on the contrary will invariably end in loss. He who comprehends this will know that he must proceed on the basis of principle and discard the factor of desire.

There is a proper way to initiate undertakings. If you estimate that the income from a particular undertaking will be large and the outlay small, then the project is practical. But a deluded ruler does not understand this. He estimates the income but not the outlay, and though the outlay may be twice the income, he fails to comprehend that this is a loss. Thus in name he appears to have profited but in fact he has not; the success is small but the loss great. An achievement can be called successful only if the income is large and the outlay small. But if men are allowed to expend large sums of money without incurring blame and still take credit for the meager successes they achieve, then the ministers will think nothing of spending large sums to accomplish a small aim. Only small gains will be achieved, and in addition the ruler will suffer loss.

Those who have no understanding of government always tell you, "Never change old ways, never depart from established custom!" But the sage cares nothing about change or no change; his only concern is to rule properly. Whether or not he changes old ways, whether or not he departs from established customs depends solely upon whether such old ways and customs are effective or not.

If Yi Yin had not changed the ways of Yin and T'ai-kung had not changed the ways of Chou, then T'ang and Wu would never have become kings. If Kuan Chung had not reformed the ways of Ch'i and Kuo Yen had not altered those of Chin, then dukes Huan and Wen would never have become dictators.[3]

In general, those who disapprove of changing old ways are simply timid about altering what the people have grown used to. But those who fail to change old ways are often in fact prolonging the course of disorder, while those who strive to gratify the people are after some selfish and evil end. If the people are too stupid to recognize the signs of disorder, and their superiors too fainthearted to adopt reforms, then government has gone awry.

The ruler of men must be enlightened enough to comprehend the way of government and strict enough to put it into effect. Though it means going against the will of the people, he will enforce his rule. In proof of this, we may note that Lord Shang, when he came and went at court, was guarded by iron spears and heavy shields to prevent sudden attack.[4] Similarly, when Kuo Yen instituted his new policies in Chin, Duke Wen provided himself with bodyguards, and when Kuan Chung first began his reforms in Ch'i, Duke Huan rode in an armored carriage. All these were precautions against

[3] Yi Yin and T'ai-kung were sage ministers who aided King T'ang, the founder of the Yin or Shang dynasty, and King Wu, the founder of the Chou, respectively. Kuan Chung (d. 645 B.C.) was adviser to Duke Huan of Ch'i (see above p. 33, n. 4). Kuo Yen, whose surname is given in other works as Kao or Hsi, performed a similar service for Duke Wen (636–628 B.C.) of Chin. These last two rulers constitute the first and second of the so-called Five *Pa*—dictators or overlords.

[4] On Lord Shang, the Legalist minister of Duke Hsiao of Ch'in, whose severe measures made him extremely unpopular with the people, see pp. 82–83 above.

danger from the people. For the people, in their stupid and slovenly way, will groan at even a small expenditure and forget the great profits to be reaped from it.[5]

[5] The section closes with a passage of 34 characters, the meaning of which is almost impossible to make out. It deals with historical anecdotes that are otherwise unknown, and in addition the text appears to be corrupt. It has seemed best, therefore, to omit it altogether.

THE FIVE VERMIN

(SECTION 49)

In the most ancient times, when men were few and creatures numerous, human beings could not overcome the birds, beasts, insects, and reptiles. Then a sage appeared who fashioned nests of wood to protect men from harm. The people were delighted and made him ruler of the world, calling him the Nest Builder. The people lived on fruits, berries, mussels, and clams—things rank and evil-smelling that hurt their bellies, so that many of them fell ill. Then a sage appeared who drilled with sticks and produced fire with which to transform the rank and putrid foods. The people were delighted and made him ruler of the world, calling him the Drill Man.

In the age of middle antiquity there was a great flood in the world, but Kun and Yü of the Hsia dynasty opened up channels for the water. In the age of recent antiquity Chieh and Chou ruled in a violent and perverse way, but T'ang of the Yin dynasty and Wu of the Chou dynasty overthrew them.

Now if anyone had built wooden nests or drilled for fire in the time of the Hsia dynasty, Kun and Yü would have laughed at him, and if anyone had tried to open channels for the water during the Yin or Chou dynasties, T'ang and Wu would have laughed at him. This being so, if people in the present age go about exalting the ways of Yao, Shun, Yü, T'ang, and Wu, the sages of today are bound to laugh at them. For the sage does not try to practice the ways of antiquity or

to abide by a fixed standard, but examines the affairs of the
age and takes what precautions are necessary.

There was a farmer of Sung who tilled the land, and in his
field was a stump. One day a rabbit, racing across the field,
bumped into the stump, broke its neck, and died. Thereupon
the farmer laid aside his plow and took up watch beside the
stump, hoping that he would get another rabbit in the same
way. But he got no more rabbits, and instead became the
laughing stock of Sung. Those who think they can take the
ways of the ancient kings and use them to govern the people
of today all belong in the category of stump-watchers!

In ancient times husbands did not have to till the fields, for
the seeds of grass and the fruit of the trees were enough for
people to eat. Wives did not have to weave, for the skins of
birds and beasts provided sufficient clothing. No one had to
struggle to keep himself supplied. The people were few, there
was an abundance of goods, and so no one quarreled. Therefore, no rich rewards were doled out, no harsh punishments
were administered, and yet the people of themselves were
orderly. But nowadays no one regards five sons as a large number, and these five sons in turn have five sons each, so that
before the grandfather has died, he has twenty-five grand-
children. Hence the number of people increases, goods grow
scarce, and men have to struggle and slave for a meager living. *Communism*
Therefore they fall to quarreling, and though rewards are
doubled and punishments are piled on, they cannot be prevented from growing disorderly.

When Yao ruled the world, he left the thatch of his roof un-
trimmed, and his speckled beams were not planed. He ate
coarse millet and a soup of greens, wore deerskin in winter
days and rough fiber robes in summer. Even a lowly gatekeeper was no worse clothed and provided for than he. When

Yü ruled the world, he took plow and spade in hand to lead his people, working until there was no more down on his thighs or hair on his shins. Even the toil of a slave taken prisoner in the wars was no bitterer than his. Therefore those men in ancient times who abdicated and relinquished the rule of the world were, in a manner of speaking, merely forsaking the life of a gatekeeper and escaping from the toil of a slave. Therefore they thought little of handing over the rule of the world to someone else. Nowadays, however, the magistrate of a district dies and his sons and grandsons are able to go riding about in carriages for generations after. Therefore people prize such offices. In the matter of relinquishing things, people thought nothing of stepping down from the position of Son of Heaven in ancient times, yet they are very reluctant to give up the post of district magistrate today; this is because of the difference in the actual benefits received.

Those who live in the mountains and must descend to the valley to fetch their water give each other gifts of water at festival time. Those who live in the swamps and are troubled by dampness actually hire laborers to dig ditches to drain off the water. In the spring following a famine year even the little boys of the family get no food; in the fall of a year of plenty even casual visitors are feasted. It is not that men are indifferent to their own flesh and blood and generous to passing visitors; it is because of the difference in the amount of food to be had.

Hence, when men of ancient times made light of material goods, it was not because they were benevolent, but because there was a surplus of goods; and when men quarrel and snatch today, it is not because they are vicious, but because goods have grown scarce. When men lightly relinquish the position of Son of Heaven, it is not because they are high-minded, but because the advantages of the post are slight; when men strive for sinecures in the government, it is not because they are base, but because the power they will acquire is great.

When the sage rules, he takes into consideration the quantity of things and deliberates on scarcity and plenty. Though his punishments may be light, this is not due to his compassion; though his penalties may be severe, this is not because he is cruel; he simply follows the custom appropriate to the time. Circumstances change according to the age, and ways of dealing with them change with the circumstances.

In ancient times King Wen lived in the area between Feng and Hao, his domain no more than a hundred *li* square, but he practiced benevolence and righteousness, won over the Western Barbarians, and eventually became ruler of the world. King Yen of Hsü lived east of the Han River in a territory five hundred *li* square. He practiced benevolence and righteousness, and thirty-six states came with gifts of territory to pay him tribute, until King Wen of Ching, fearing for his own safety, called out his troops, attacked Hsü, and wiped it out.[1] Thus King Wen practiced benevolence and righteousness and became ruler of the world, but King Yen practiced benevolence and righteousness and destroyed his state. This is because benevolence and righteousness served for ancient times, but no longer serve today. So I say that circumstances differ with the age.

In the time of Shun the Miao tribes were unsubmissive, and Yü proposed to attack them. But Shun said, "That will not do! To take up arms while the virtue of the ruler is not

[1] The story of King Yen of Hsü appears in many different forms in early works. Because there is so much disagreement on the facts, it is impossible to assign the events to any particular date, or even to determine whether they have any basis in historical fact.

perfected would be a violation of the Way." Shun taught the ways of good government for the following three years, and then took up shield and battle-ax and performed the war dance, and the Miao submitted. But in the war with the Kung-kung,[2] men used iron lances with steel heads that reached to the enemy, so that unless one was protected by a stout helmet and armor he was likely to be wounded. Hence shields and battle-axes served for ancient times, but no longer serve today. So I say that as circumstances change the ways of dealing with them alter too.

Men of high antiquity strove for moral virtue; men of middle times sought out wise schemes; men of today vie to be known for strength and spirit. Ch'i was once planning an attack on Lu. Lu dispatched Tzu-kung[3] to dissuade the men of Ch'i, but they replied, "Your words are eloquent enough. But what we want is territory, and that is the one thing you have not mentioned." So in the end Ch'i called out its troops, attacked Lu, and fixed its boundary line only ten *li* away from the Lu capital gate.

King Yen practiced benevolence and righteousness and the state of Hsü was wiped out; Tzu-kung employed eloquence and wisdom and Lu lost territory. So it is obvious that benevolence, righteousness, eloquence, and wisdom are not the means by which to maintain the state. Discard the benevolence of King Yen and put an end to Tzu-kung's wisdom; build up the might of Hsü and Lu until they can stand face to face with

---

[2] Kung-kung is usually mentioned as a legendary figure of the time of Yao or earlier, but Han Fei Tzu apparently has some other meaning of the name in mind. Perhaps Kung-kung here refers to a tribe that traced its ancestry back to the figure of that name.

[3] Tzu-kung was a disciple of Confucius noted for his eloquence. The *Tso chuan*, Duke Ai, 15th year, mentions his mission to Ch'i in 480 B.C., but the rest of the anecdote appears to be apocryphal.

a state of ten thousand war chariots—then Ch'i and Ching will no longer be able to do with them as they please!

Past and present have different customs; new and old adopt different measures. To try to use the ways of a generous and lenient government to rule the people of a critical age is like trying to drive a runaway horse without using reins or whip. This is the misfortune that ignorance invites.

Now the Confucians and Mo-ists all praise the ancient kings for their universal love of the world, saying that they looked after the people as parents look after a beloved child.[4] And how do they prove this contention? They say, "Whenever the minister of justice administered some punishment, the ruler would purposely cancel all musical performances; and whenever the ruler learned that the death sentence had been passed on someone, he would shed tears." For this reason they praise the ancient kings.

Now if ruler and subject must become like father and son before there can be order, then we must suppose that there is no such thing as an unruly father or son. Among human affections none takes priority over the love of parents for their children. But though all parents may show love for their children, the children are not always well behaved. And though the parents may love them even more, will this prevent the children from becoming unruly? Now the love of the ancient kings for their people was no greater than the love of parents for their children. And if such love cannot prevent children from becoming unruly, then how can it bring the people to order?

As for the ruler's shedding tears when punishments are carried out in accordance with the law—this is a fine display

---

[4] Supplying the words *chih ai tzu* in accordance with the suggestion of Ch'en Ch'i-yu.

of benevolence but contributes nothing to the achievement of order. Benevolence may make one shed tears and be reluctant to apply penalties; but law makes it clear that such penalties must be applied. The ancient kings allowed law to be supreme and did not give in to their tearful longings. Hence it is obvious that benevolence cannot be used to achieve order in the state.

Moreover, the people will bow naturally to authority, but few of them can be moved by righteousness. Confucius was one of the greatest sages of the world. He perfected his conduct, made clear the Way, and traveled throughout the area within the four seas, but in all that area those who rejoiced in his benevolence, admired his righteousness, and were willing to become his disciples numbered only seventy. For to honor benevolence is a rare thing, and to adhere to righteousness is hard. Therefore within the vast area of the world only seventy men became his disciples, and only one man—he himself—was truly benevolent and righteous.

Duke Ai of Lu was a mediocre ruler, yet when he ascended the throne and faced south as sovereign of the state, there was no one within its boundaries who did not acknowledge allegiance to him. The people will bow naturally to authority, and he who wields authority may easily command men to submit; therefore Confucius remained a subject and Duke Ai continued to be his ruler. It was not that Confucius was won by the duke's righteousness; he simply bowed before his authority. On the basis of righteousness alone, Confucius would never have bowed before Duke Ai; but because the duke wielded authority, he was able to make Confucius acknowledge his sovereignty.

Nowadays, when scholars counsel a ruler, they do not urge him to wield authority, which is the certain way to success,

but instead insist that he must practice benevolence and
righteousness before he can become a true king. This is, in
effect, to demand that the ruler rise to the level of Confucius,
and that all the ordinary people of the time be like Confucius'
disciples. Such a policy is bound to fail.

Now here is a young man of bad character. His parents rail
at him but he does not reform; the neighbors scold but he is
unmoved; his teachers instruct him but he refuses to change
his ways. Thus, although three fine influences are brought
to bear on him—the love of his parents, the efforts of the
neighbors, the wisdom of his teachers—yet he remains unmoved and refuses to change so much as a hair on his shin.
But let the local magistrate send out the government soldiers
to enforce the law and search for evil-doers, and then he is
filled with terror, reforms his conduct, and changes his ways.
Thus the love of parents is not enough to make children
learn what is right, but must be backed up by the strict penalties of the local officials; for people by nature grow proud on
love, but they listen to authority.

Even the nimble Lou-chi could not climb a city wall ten
spans high, because it is too precipitous; but lame sheep may
easily graze up and down a mountain a hundred times as
high, because the slope is gradual. Therefore the enlightened
ruler makes his laws precipitous and his punishments severe.
Ordinary people are unwilling to discard a few feet of cloth,
but even Robber Chih would not pick up a hundred taels of
molten gold. As long as there is no harm involved, people
will not discard a few feet of cloth, but because they are
certain to hurt their hands they refuse to pick up a hundred
taels of molten gold. Therefore the enlightened ruler makes
his punishments certain.

For this reason, the best rewards are those which are generous and predictable, so that the people may profit by them. The best penalties are those which are severe and inescapable, so that the people will fear them. The best laws are those which are uniform and inflexible, so that the people can understand them. Therefore the ruler should never delay in handing out rewards, nor be merciful in administering punishments. If praise accompanies the reward, and censure follows on the heels of punishment, then worthy and unworthy men alike will put forth their best efforts.

But this is not the way things are done at present. The rulers hand out official titles to men who have achieved merit but assign them to insignificant posts. They give rewards to the farmers but in practice actually reduce their means of livelihood. They dissociate themselves from those who spurn official position but at the same time praise their contempt for the world. They punish those who violate the prohibitions but at the same time admire their bravery. Thus the things which they censure or praise are completely at odds with those which they reward or punish.

Nowadays, he who makes certain to avenge any wrong done to his brother is called an upright man, and he who joins his friend in attacking the perpetrator of an insult is called a man of honor. Such a man performs deeds that are regarded as upright and honorable, and in doing so violates the laws and prohibitions of the ruler. But the ruler, lost in admiration for such upright and honorable deeds, forgets to punish the violation of his laws, and hence the people outdo each other in shows of valor and the magistrates can no longer control them.

Likewise, he who manages to get clothing and food without working for them is called an able man, and he who wins esteem without having achieved any merit in battle is called a worthy man. But the deeds of such able and worthy men actually weaken the army and bring waste to the land. If the ruler rejoices in the deeds of such men, and forgets the harm they do by weakening the army and bringing waste to the land, then private interests will prevail and public profit will come to naught.

The Confucians with their learning bring confusion to the law; the knights with their military prowess violate the prohibitions.[5] Yet the ruler treats both groups with respect, and so we have disorder. People who deviate from the law should be treated as criminals, and yet the scholars actually attain posts in the government because of their literary accomplishments. People who violate the prohibitions ought to be punished, and yet the bands of knights are able to make a living by wielding their swords in a private cause. Hence, those whom the law condemns, the ruler accepts, and those whom the magistrates seek to punish, the higher officials patronize. Thus law and practice, high official and lowly magistrate, are all set at odds, and there is no fixed standard. Under such circumstances even ten Yellow Emperors could not bring the state to order. Those who practice benevolence and righteousness should not be praised, for to praise them is to cast aspersion on military achievements; men of literary accomplishment should not be employed in the government, for to employ them is to bring confusion to the law.

In the state of Ch'u there was a man named Honest Kung. When his father stole a sheep, he reported the theft to the

---

[5] When the Confucians wished to oppose some political measure, they customarily declared that it was not in accord with ancient practice and cited some early text in proof. The knights or cavaliers, noted for their daring and strict code of honor, often acted as local "bosses" in defiance of the government authorities, guaranteeing protection to people who sought their aid or hiring out their services in the conduct of private vendettas.

authorities. But the local magistrate, considering that the man was honest in the service of his sovereign but a villain to his own father, replied, "Put him to death!", and the man was accordingly sentenced and executed. Thus we see that a man who is an honest subject of his sovereign may be an infamous son to his father.

There was a man of Lu who accompanied his sovereign to war. Three times he went into battle, and three times he ran away. When Confucius asked him the reason, he replied, "I have an aged father and, if I should die, there would be no one to take care of him." Confucius, considering the man filial, recommended him and had him promoted to a post in the government. Thus we see that a man who is a filial son to his father may be a traitorous subject to his lord.

The magistrate of Ch'u executed a man, and as a result the felonies of the state were never reported to the authorities; Confucius rewarded a man, and as a result the people of Lu thought nothing of surrendering or running away in battle. Since the interests of superior and inferior are as disparate as all this, it is hopeless for the ruler to praise the actions of the private individual and at the same time try to insure blessing to the state's altars of the soil and grain.

In ancient times when Ts'ang Chieh created the system of writing, he used the character for "private" to express the idea of self-centeredness, and combined the elements for "private" and "opposed to" to form the character for "public." The fact that public and private are mutually opposed was already well understood at the time of Ts'ang Chieh. To regard the two as being identical in interest is a disaster which comes from lack of consideration.

If I were to give advice from the point of view of the private individual, I would say the best thing is to practice benevolence[6] and righteousness and cultivate the literary arts. By practicing benevolence and righteousness, you become trusted, and when you have become trusted you may receive official appointment. Similarly, by cultivating the literary arts you may become an eminent teacher, and when you have become an eminent teacher you will win honor and renown. This is the highest goal of the private individual. But when this happens, then, from the point of view of the state, someone who has performed no meritorious service to the nation is receiving official appointment, and someone who holds no government title is enjoying honor and renown. If the government is conducted in this fashion, then the state will face certain disorder and the ruler will surely be in peril. Hence the interests of the state and the individual are mutually at odds, and both cannot prevail at the same time.

not that! anything but..

To reward those who cut off the heads of the enemy and yet to admire acts of mercy and compassion; to hand out titles and stipends to those who capture the enemy's cities and yet to give ear to doctrines of universal[7] love; to strengthen one's armor and sharpen one's weapons in preparation for the time of trouble, and yet praise the elegant attire of the civil gentry; to hope to enrich the nation through agriculture and ward off the enemy with trained soldiers, and yet to pay honor to men of literary accomplishment; to spurn those people who respect their rulers and fear the law, and instead to patronize the bands of wandering knights and private swordsmen—to indulge in contradictory acts like these is to insure that the state will never be well ordered. The nation at peace may patronize Confucian scholars and cavaliers; but the nation in danger must call upon its fighting men. Thus those who are

---

[6] Reading *jen* instead of *hsing* here and in the clause following.
[7] Reading *chien* instead of *lien*.

of real profit to the state are not used and those who are used are of no profit. As a result, those who attend to government business become careless in their jobs and wandering scholars increase in number day by day. Hence the disorder of our age.

The world calls worthy those whose conduct is marked by integrity and good faith, and wise those whose words are subtle and mysterious. But even the wisest man has difficulty understanding words that are subtle and mysterious. Now if you want to set up laws for the masses and you try to base them on doctrines that even the wisest men have difficulty in understanding, how can the common people comprehend them? A man who cannot even get his fill of the coarsest grain does not insist on meat and fine millet; a man with a short coat all in rags does not insist on waiting for embroidered robes. It is the same in government affairs; if you cannot find the solution to critical problems, you have no business worrying about unimportant ones. Now in administering your rule and dealing with the people, if you do not speak in terms that any man and woman can plainly understand, but long to apply the doctrines of the wise men, then you will defeat your own efforts at rule. Subtle and mysterious words are no business of the people.

If people regard [8] those who act with integrity and good faith as worthy, it must be because they value[9] men who have no deceit, and they value men of no deceit because they themselves have no means to protect themselves from deceit. The common people in selecting their friends, for example, have no wealth by which to win others over, and no authority by which to intimidate others. For that reason they seek for men who are without deceit to be their friends. But the ruler oc-

---

[8] Omitting the *liang*, which is superfluous.

[9] Following texts which read *kuei* at the beginning of this clause.

cupies a position whereby he may impose his will upon others, and he has the whole wealth of the nation at his disposal; he may dispense lavish rewards and severe penalties and, by wielding these two handles, may illuminate all things through his wise policies.[10] In that case, even traitorous ministers like T'ien Ch'ang and Tzu-han would not dare to deceive him.[11] Why should he have to wait for men who are by nature not deceitful?

Hardly ten men of true integrity and good faith can be found today, and yet the offices of the state number in the hundreds. If they must be filled by men of integrity and good faith, then there will never be enough men to go around; and if the offices are left unfilled, then those whose business it is to govern will dwindle in numbers while disorderly men increase. Therefore the way of the enlightened ruler is to unify the laws instead of seeking for wise men, to lay down firm policies instead of longing for men of good faith. Hence his laws never fail him, and there is no felony or deceit among his officials.

These days, when the ruler listens to men's words, he delights in their eloquence and does not bother to inquire if they are apt, and when he embarks upon some undertaking, he is thrilled by the report of what is to be accomplished and does not demand to see actual results. For this reason the people of the world, when they come to make a speech, strive for eloquence and disregard the question of whether their words are practical. Hence the court is filled with men discoursing on the former kings and discussing benevolence and righteousness, and the government cannot escape disorder. Likewise, in the matter of personal conduct, men try to outdo

[10] The text of the last part of the sentence appears to be corrupt and the translation is tentative.

[11] For T'ien Ch'ang and Tzu-han, see above, p. 31.

each other in high-minded deeds, regardless of whether they produce any useful results. Hence, men of wisdom retire from government service and go off to live in caves, refusing the stipends that are offered them, and as a result the armies grow weaker and the government cannot escape disorder. What is the cause of all this? The fact that what the people praise and the ruler honors are actually policies that lead to the ruin of the state.

Now the people of the state all discuss good government, and everyone has a copy of the works on law by Shang Yang and Kuan Chung in his house,[12] and yet the state gets poorer and poorer, for though many people talk about farming, very few put their hands to a plow. The people of the state all discuss military affairs, and everyone has a copy of the works of Sun Wu and Wu Ch'i in his house,[13] and yet the armies grow weaker and weaker, for though many people talk about war, very few buckle on armor. Therefore an enlightened ruler will make use of men's strength but will not heed their words, will reward their accomplishments but will prohibit useless activities. Then the people will be willing to exert themselves to the point of death in the service of their sovereign.

Farming requires a lot of hard work but people will do it because they say, "This way we can get rich." War is a dangerous undertaking but people will take part in it because they say, "This way we can become eminent." Now if men who devote themselves to literature or study the art of persuasive speaking are able to get the fruits of wealth without the hard work of the farmer, and can gain the advantages of eminence without the danger of battle, then who will not take up such pursuits? So for every man who works with his hands

---

[12] The *Book of Lord Shang* and the *Kuan Tzu*, Legalist works which stressed the importance of agriculture.

[13] The *Sun Tzu* and *Wu Tzu*, works on military science.

there will be a hundred devoting themselves to the pursuit of wisdom. If those who pursue wisdom are numerous, the laws will be defeated, and if those who labor with their hands are few, the state will grow poor. Hence the age will become disordered.

Therefore, in the state of an enlightened ruler there are no books written on bamboo slips; law supplies the only instruction. There are no sermons on the former kings; the officials serve as the only teachers. There are no fierce feuds of private swordsmen; cutting off the heads of the enemy is the only deed of valor. Hence, when the people of such a state make a speech, they say nothing that is in contradiction to the law; when they act, it is in some way that will bring useful results; and when they do brave deeds, they do them in the army. Therefore, in times of peace the state is rich, and in times of trouble its armies are strong. These are what are called the resources of the ruler. The ruler must store them up, and then wait for an opening to strike at his enemy. He who would surpass the Five Emperors of antiquity and rival the Three Kings must proceed by this method.

But this is not the way things are now. Within the state the people behave as they please, while the speechmakers work to spread their influence abroad. With those at home and abroad both up to mischief and hoping for the intervention of powerful enemy states, how can the state escape danger? When the ministers speak on foreign affairs, they are either acting as spokesmen for the Horizontal or Vertical alliances[14] or trying to enlist the aid of the state to avenge some personal

[14] The Horizontal Alliance was an east-west alignment of states under the leadership of the powerful state of Ch'in in the west. The Vertical Alliance, a north-south alignment, was designed to preserve the independence of the weaker states and block Ch'in's expansion. Smaller states frequently changed their alliance according to the political expedience of the moment.

wrong. But neither the Vertical Alliance, in which one joins with a number of weak states in hopes of attacking a strong one, nor the Horizontal Alliance, in which one serves a strong state for the purpose of attacking a number of weak ones, can insure the survival of one's own state.

Those ministers who urge the Horizontal Alliance all say, "If we do not enter the service of a powerful state, we will be attacked by enemies and will face disaster!" Now when you enter the service of a powerful state, you cannot yet be certain of the practical advantages, and yet you must hand over all the maps of your territory and present your official seals when you request military aid. Once the maps have been presented, you will be stripped of territory, and once your official seals have been put into the hands of another, your prestige will vanish. If your territory is stripped away, the state will be weakened, and if your prestige vanishes, the government will fall into disorder. So you gain no benefit by entering the Horizontal Alliance in the service of a powerful state, but merely lose territory and undermine the government.

Those ministers who urge the Vertical Alliance all say, "If we do not rescue the smaller states and attack the powerful one, the whole world will be lost and, when the rest of the world is lost, our own state will be in peril and our ruler will face contempt!" Now you are not yet certain that you can actually save the smaller states, and yet you must call out your troops and face a powerful enemy. When you try to save the smaller states, you cannot always be sure of preserving them from destruction; and when you face a powerful enemy,[15] you cannot always be sure that your allies will remain loyal. And if your allies break with you, you will be at the mercy of the powerful state. Then if you send out troops to battle, your

---

[15] Reading *ti* instead of *chiao*.

armies will be defeated, and if you withdraw and try to protect your own realm, your cities will fall. So you gain no benefit by entering the Vertical Alliance in an attempt to save the smaller states, but lose your own lands and destroy your own army.

Hence, if you enter the service of a powerful state, it will dispatch its own men of authority to take over the offices in your government; and if you work to rescue the smaller states, your own important ministers will take advantage of the situation to further their interests abroad. No benefit will come to the state as a whole, but only fiefs and rich rewards for its ministers. They will enjoy all the honor, while the ruler is despised; their families will grow rich, while the state is stripped of its lands. If their schemes succeed, they will use their power to prolong their eminence; if their schemes fail, they will retire with all their wealth intact.

But if the ruler, when he heeds such urgings, honors his ministers and rewards them with titles and stipends before their advice has produced successful results, and fails to punish them when it has proved unsuccessful, then who among the wandering theorists will not come forward with some hit-or-miss scheme in hopes of benefiting by a stroke of luck?

Why do the rulers listen to the wild theories of the speech-makers, and bring destruction to the state and ruin to themselves? Because they do not distinguish clearly between public and private interests, do not examine the aptness of the words they hear, and do not make certain that punishments are meted out where they are deserved.

Each ruler says, "By attending to foreign affairs I can perhaps become a king, and if not I will at least ensure security for myself." A true king is one who is in a position to attack others, and a ruler whose state is secure cannot be attacked. But a powerful ruler can also attack others, and a ruler whose state is well ordered likewise cannot be attacked. Neither power nor order, however, can be sought abroad—they are wholly a matter of internal government. Now if the ruler does not apply the proper laws and procedures within his state, but stakes all on the wisdom of his foreign policy, his state will never become powerful and well ordered.

The proverb says, "If you have long sleeves, you'll be good at dancing; if you have lots of money, you'll be good at business." This means that it is easy to become skillful when you have ample resources. Hence, it is easy to scheme for a state that is powerful and orderly but difficult to make any plan for one that is weak and chaotic. Those who scheme for the state of Ch'in can make ten changes and still their plans will seldom fail; but those who plan for the state of Yen can scarcely make one change and still hope for success. It is not that those who plan for Ch'in are necessarily wise and those who plan for Yen are stupid—it is simply that the resources they have to work with—order in one case, disorder in the other—are different.

Chou deserted the side of Ch'in and joined the Vertical Alliance, and within a year it had lost everything.[16] Wey turned its back on Wei to join the Horizontal Alliance, and in half a year it was ruined.[17] Thus Chou was ruined by the Vertical Alliance and Wey was destroyed by the Horizontal Alliance. Instead of being so hasty in their plans to join an alliance, they should have worked to strengthen the order

[16] In 256 B.C. King Nan of the Chou dynasty joined with the leaders of the Vertical Alliance in an attack on Ch'in which failed miserably. To make amends, he was obliged the same year to turn over all his territory to Ch'in.

[17] The event to which Han Fei Tzu is probably referring occurred in 241 B.C., though the details are not known. The names of the two states are romanized the same way in modern Chinese, but I have spelled the name of the older state "Wey" to distinguish them.

within their domains, to make their laws clear and their rewards and punishments certain, to utilize the full resources of the land in building up stores of provisions, and to train their people to defend the cities to the point of death, thus ensuring that any other ruler would gain little profit by trying to seize their lands, but on the contrary would suffer great injury if he attempted to attack their states. In that case, even the ruler of a state of ten thousand war chariots would have been unwilling to wear out his armies before their strong walls and, in his exhausted condition, invite the attack of powerful enemies. This would have been the way to escape destruction. To abandon a way which assures escape from destruction, and follow instead a path that leads to certain downfall, is the greatest error one can make in governing a state. Once the wisdom of its foreign[18] policy is exhausted and its internal government has fallen into disorder, no state can be saved from ruin.

The people, in planning for their welfare, are most concerned in finding security and profit and avoiding danger and poverty. But if they must go off to fight foreign wars for the state, they face death at the hands of the enemy should they advance and death from official punishment should they retreat—hence they are in danger. If they must abandon their domestic affairs and go off to endure the sweat and hardship of battle, their families will grow poor and the ruler is likely never to reward them for their services—hence they face poverty. If such poverty and danger lie before them, how can you expect the people not to try to escape them? So they flock to the gates of influential men seeking a guarantee of exemption from military service, for with such a guarantee they may stay far from the scene of battle and live in safety.

---

[18] Reversing the position of the *nei* and *wai*.

Likewise they slip bribes to the men in office in order to get some appointment, for with such an appointment they may insure their private security. If they can obtain anything so profitable as private security, how can you expect them not to resort to such measures? Hence men who are concerned with public welfare grow fewer, and those who think only of private interests increase in number.

An enlightened ruler will administer his state in such a way as to decrease the number of merchants, artisans, and other men who make their living by wandering from place to place, and will see to it that such men are looked down upon. In this way he lessens the number of people who abandon[19] primary pursuits [i.e., agriculture] to take up secondary occupations. Nowadays, however, if a man can enlist the private pleading of someone at court, he can buy offices and titles. When offices and titles can be bought, you may be sure that merchants and artisans will not remain despised for long; and when wealth and money, no matter how dishonestly gotten, can buy what is in the market, you may be sure that the number of merchants will not remain small for long. When a man who sits back and collects taxes makes twice as much as the farmer and enjoys greater honor than the plowman or the soldier, then public-spirited men will grow few and merchants and tradesmen will increase in number.

These are the customs of a disordered state: Its scholars praise the ways of the former kings and imitate their benevolence and righteousness, put on a fair appearance and speak in elegant phrases, thus casting doubt upon the laws of the time and causing the ruler to be of two minds. Its speechmakers[20] propound false schemes and borrow influence from

[19] Reading *she* instead of *ch'ü*.
[20] Reading *t'an* instead of *ku*.

abroad, furthering their private interests and forgetting the welfare of the state's altars of the soil and grain. Its swordsmen gather bands of followers about them and perform deeds of honor, making a fine name for themselves and violating the prohibitions of the five government bureaus. Those of its people who are worried about military service[21] flock to the gates of private individuals and pour out their wealth in bribes to influential men who will plead for them, in this way escaping the hardship of battle. Its merchants and artisans spend their time making articles of no practical use and gathering stores of luxury goods, accumulating riches, waiting for the best time to sell, and exploiting the farmers.

These five groups are the vermin of the state. If the rulers do not wipe out such vermin, and in their place encourage men of integrity and public spirit, then they should not be surprised, when they look about the area within the four seas, to see states perish and ruling houses wane and die.

[21] Reading *yi* instead of *yü*.

EMINENCE IN LEARNING

(SECTION 50)

In the present age, the Confucians and Mo-ists are well
known for their learning. The Confucians pay the highest
honor to Confucius, the Mo-ists to Mo Ti. Since the death of
Confucius, the Tzu-chang School, the Tzu-ssu School, the Yen
Family School, the Meng Family School, the Ch'i-tiao Family
School, the Chung-liang Family School, the Sun Family
School, and the Yüeh-cheng Family School have appeared.
Since the death of Mo Tzu, the Hsiang-li Family School, the
Hsiang-fu Family School, and the Teng-ling Family School
have appeared. Thus, since the death of its founder, the Confucian school has split into eight factions, and the Mo-ist school
into three. Their doctrines and practices are different or even
contradictory, and yet each claims to represent the true teaching of Confucius and Mo Tzu. But since we cannot call Confucius and Mo Tzu back to life, who is to decide which of the
present versions of the doctrine is the right one?

Confucius and Mo Tzu both followed the ways of Yao and
Shun, and though their practices differed, each claimed to be
following the real Yao and Shun.[1] But since we cannot call
Yao and Shun back to life, who is to decide whether it is the
Confucians or the Mo-ists who are telling the truth?

Now over seven hundred years have passed since Yin and
early Chou times, and over two thousand years since Yü and

[1] Judging from the *Analects*, Confucius himself had little to say about
the ancient sage rulers Yao and Shun, and the few references to them may
well be later insertions in the text. But Confucian scholars of late Chou
times paid great honor to Yao and Shun and compiled the "Canon of
Yao," the first section of the *Book of Documents,* as a record of their lives.

early Hsia times. If we cannot even decide which of the present versions of Confucian and Mo-ist doctrine are the genuine ones, how can we hope to scrutinize the ways of Yao and Shun, who lived three thousands years ago? Obviously we can be sure of nothing! He who claims to be sure of something for which there is no evidence is a fool, and he who acts on the basis of what cannot be proved is an imposter. Hence it is clear that those who claim to follow the ancient kings and to be able to describe with certainty the ways of Yao and Shun must be either fools or imposters. The learning of fools and impostors, doctrines that are motley and contradictory—such things as these the enlightened ruler will never accept.

For funerals, the Mo-ists prescribe that winter mourning garments be worn in winter and summer garments in summer, that the coffin be of paulownia wood three inches thick, and that mourning be observed for three months. The rulers of the time regard such ways as frugal and honor them. The Confucians, on the other hand, will bankrupt the family to carry out a funeral, wearing mourning garments for three years, reducing themselves to physical exhaustion and walking about with canes. The rulers of the time regard such ways as filial and honor them. Now if you approve of the frugality of Mo Tzu, you must condemn Confucius for his extravagance, and if you approve of the filial piety of Confucius, you must condemn Mo Tzu for his impiety. Thus the teachings of the Confucians and Mo-ists embrace both piety and impiety, extravagance and frugality, and yet the ruler honors them both!

According to the teaching of Ch'i-tiao,[2] a man should never

---

[2] Nothing is known of the identity of this man. He appears to be a different person from the Ch'i-tiao mentioned above as the leader of one school of Confucianism.

cringe before others or flinch in the face of danger; if his actions are base, he should not refuse to be treated as a slave, but if his actions are upright, he should not hesitate to defy the feudal lords. The rulers of the time regard such conduct as honorable and praise it. According to the teaching of Sung Jung-tzu,[3] a man should condemn warfare and contention and refuse to take part in acts of vengeance; he should not be embarrassed to go to jail and should consider it no shame to suffer insult. The rulers of the time regard such an attitude as broad-minded and praise it. Now if you approve of the honorable conduct of Ch'i-tiao, you must condemn Sung Jung for being too forgiving, and if you approve of the broad-mindedness of Sung Jung, you must condemn Ch'i-tiao for being too violent. Thus these two codes of behavior embrace both broad-mindedness and a keen sense of honor, forgiveness and violence, and yet the ruler honors them both!

Because the ruler gives equal ear to the learning of fools and impostors and the wranglings of the motley and contradictory schools, the gentlemen of the world follow no fixed policy in their words and no constant code of action in their behavior. As ice and live coals cannot share the same container for long, or winter and summer both arrive at the same time, so, too, motley and contradictory doctrines cannot stand side by side and produce a state of order. If equal ear is given to motley doctrines, false codes of behavior, and contradictory assertions, how can there be anything but chaos? If the ruler listens and acts in such a way, he will surely govern his people in the same absurd fashion.

When the scholars of today discuss good government, many of them say, "Give land to the poor and destitute so that those

---

[3] Referred to in other texts as Sung Chien or Sung K'eng, he seems to have taught a doctrine of passivity, frugality, and few desires.

who have no means of livelihood may be provided for." Now if men start out with equal opportunities and yet there are a few who, without the help of unusually good harvests or outside income, are able to keep themselves well supplied, it must be due either to hard work or to frugal living. If men start out with equal opportunities and yet there are a few who, without having suffered from some calamity like famine or sickness, still sink into poverty and destitution, it must be due either to laziness or to extravagant living. The lazy and extravagant grow poor; the diligent and frugal get rich. Now if the ruler levies money from the rich in order to give alms to the poor, he is robbing the diligent and frugal and indulging the lazy and extravagant. If he expects by such means to induce the people to work industriously and spend with caution, he will be disappointed.

Now suppose there is a man who on principle refuses to enter a city that is in danger, to take part in a military campaign, or in fact to change so much as a hair of his shin, though it might bring the greatest benefit to the world.[4] The rulers of the time are sure to honor him, admiring his wisdom, praising his conduct, and regarding him as a man who despises material things and values his life. Now the ruler hands out good fields and large houses and offers titles and stipends in order to encourage the people to risk their lives in his service. But if he honors and praises a man who despises material things and values life above everything else, and at the same time expects the people to risk their lives and serve him to the death, he will be disappointed.

Then there are other men who collect books, study rhetoric,

A reference to the followers of Yang Chu. Cf. *Mencius* VIIA, 26: "Mencius said, 'The principle of Yang Tzu was "each one for himself." Though he might have benefited the whole world by plucking out a single hair, he would not have done it.'"

gather bands of disciples, and devote themselves to literature, learning, and debate. The rulers of the time are sure to treat them with respect, saying, "It is the way of the former kings to honor worthy men." The farmers are the ones who must pay taxes to the officials, and yet the ruler patronizes scholars —thus the farmer's taxes grow heavier and heavier, while the scholars enjoy increasing reward. If the ruler hopes, in spite of this, that the people will work industriously and spend little time talking, he will be disappointed.

There are others who establish a name for chivalrous action and gather bands of followers, who guard their honor from all insult and avenge with ready swords the slightest sullen word that reaches their ears. The rulers of the time are sure to treat such men with courtesy, considering them gentlemen of self-respect. No reward is given to those who strive to cut off the heads of the enemy in battle, and yet the daring that men show in their family feuds brings them honor and renown. If the ruler hopes, in spite of this, that the people will fight fiercely to drive back the enemy and refrain from private quarrels, he will be disappointed. The nation at peace may patronize Confucian scholars and cavaliers, but the nation in danger must call upon its fighting men. Thus those who are patronized are not those who are of real use, and those who are of real use are not those who are patronized. Hence we have disorder.

Moreover, when the ruler listens to a scholar, if he approves of his words, he should give them official dissemination and appoint the man to a post; but if he disapproves of his words, he should dismiss the man and put a stop to his teaching. Now, though the ruler may approve of some doctrine, he does not give it official dissemination, and though he may disapprove of some doctrine, he does not put a stop to it. Not to use what you approve of and not to suppress what you disapprove of—this is the way to confusion and ruin.

T'an-t'ai Tzu-yü had the appearance of a gentleman. Confucius, considering him promising, accepted him as a disciple but, after associating with him for some time, he found that his actions did not come up to his looks. Ts'ai Yü's speech was elegant and refined and Confucius, considering him promising, accepting him as a disciple. But after associating with him, he found that his wisdom did not match his eloquence. Therefore Confucius said, "Should I choose a man on the basis of looks? I made a mistake with Tzu-yü. Should I choose a man on the basis of his speech? I made a mistake with Ts'ai Yü." Thus even Confucius, for all his wisdom, had to admit that he judged the facts wrongly. Now our new orators today are far more voluble than Ts'ai Yü, and the rulers of the age far more susceptible to delusion than Confucius. If they appoint men to office simply because they are pleased with their words, how can they fail to make mistakes?

Wei trusted the eloquence of Meng Mao and met with calamity below Mount Hua.[5] Chao trusted the eloquence of Ma-fu and encountered disaster at Ch'ang-p'ing.[6] These two instances show what mistakes can be made by trusting men because of their eloquence.

If one were only to note the quantity of tin used in the alloy, examine the color of the metal, but apply no other test, then even the famous Smithy Ou could not guarantee the sharpness of a sword. But if one sees it strike off the heads of water birds and cut down horses on land, then even the stupidest slave would not doubt that the sword is sharp. If

[5] In 273 B.C. Ch'in attacked Wei and its allies, defeating and routing the army of the Wei general Meng Mao at Hua-yang.

[6] The Chao general Chao Ma-fu was defeated at Ch'ang-p'ing by the Ch'in army in 260 B.C.

one were only to look at a horse's teeth and examine[7] its shape, then even the famous judge of horses, Po Lo, could not guarantee the quality of the horse. But if one hitches it to a carriage and observes how it covers a certain distance of ground, then even the stupidest slave can tell whether the horse is good or not. Similarly, if one were only to observe a man's features and dress and listen to his speech, then even Confucius could not be certain what kind of person he is. But if one tries him out in government office and examines his achievements, then even a man of mediocre judgment can tell whether he is stupid or wise.

In the bureaucracy of an enlightened ruler the prime minister has come up from the post of district magistrate and the renowned generals have risen from the ranks. Since achievements are invariably rewarded, the able man rises in title and stipend and works harder than ever; since he keeps moving to a higher office and a better rank, he will in time reach an important position and do his job better than ever. Thus to see to it that titles and stipends are generous[8] and jobs are well done is the way of a true king.

The ruler with a thousand *li* of rocky land cannot be called rich; the ruler with a million funerary dolls cannot be called powerful. It is not that the stony fields are not vast or the dolls not numerous. But such a ruler cannot be called rich or powerful because stony fields will grow no grain and dolls will not fend off an enemy. Now the artists and craftsmen, or the merchants who buy themselves government offices, manage to eat without tilling the land. Thus the land remains as unproductive as though it were in fact a stony

[7] Supplying *hsiang* above *hsing*.

[8] Reading *hou* instead of *ta* in accordance with the suggestion of Ch'en Ch'i-yu.

field. Likewise the Confucians and cavaliers gain fame and glory without the hardships of service in the army; they are in fact useless citizens, no different from funerary dolls. Now if you recognize the curse[9] of having only stony lands and lifeless dolls, but not the curse of merchants who buy their way into office, or Confucians and cavaliers—men who till no land and serve no purpose—then you have no head for analogies.

Although the ruler of a state whose power is equal to yours may admire your righteousness, you cannot force him to come with tribute and acknowledge your sovereignty; but although one of the marquises within your borders may disapprove of your actions, you can make him bring the customary gifts and attend your court. Thus he who has great power at his disposal may force others to pay him court, but he whose power is weak must pay court to others. For this reason the enlightened ruler works to build up power. In a strict household there are no unruly slaves, but the children of a kindly mother often turn out bad. From this I know that power and authority can prevent violence, but kindness and generosity are insufficient to put an end to disorder.

When a sage rules the state, he does not depend on people's doing good of themselves; he sees to it that they are not allowed to do what is bad. If he depends on people's doing good of themselves, then within his borders he can count less than ten instances of success. But if he sees to it that they are not allowed to do what is bad, then the whole state can be brought to a uniform level of order. Those who rule must employ measures that will be effective with the majority and discard those that will be effective with only a few. Therefore they devote themselves not to virtue but to law.

[9] Reversing the order of *huo* and *chih*.

If you depend on arrow shafts' becoming straight of themselves, you will never produce one arrow in a hundred generations. If you depend on pieces of wood's becoming round of themselves, you will never get a cartwheel in a thousand years. If in a hundred generations you never find such a thing as an arrow shaft that makes itself straight or a piece of wood that makes itself round, then how it is that people all manage to ride around in carriages and shoot down birds? Because the tools of straightening and bending are used. And even if, without the application of such tools, there were an arrow shaft that made itself straight or a piece of wood that made itself round, a good craftsman would not prize it. Why? Because it is not only one man who wants to ride, and not just one shot that the archer wants to make. And even if, without depending upon rewards and punishments, there were a man who became good of himself, the enlightened ruler would not prize him. Why? Because the laws of the state must not be ignored, and it is more than one man who must be governed. Therefore a ruler who understands policy does not pursue fortuitous goodness, but follows the way of certain success.

If someone were to go around telling people, "I can give you wisdom and long life!", then the world would regard him as an impostor. Wisdom is a matter of man's nature, and long life is a matter of fate, and neither human nature nor fate can be got from others. Because the man tells people he can do what is impossible, the world naturally considers him an impostor. To say you can do something which you cannot do is simply to make an empty assertion, and an empty assertion cannot affect human nature.[10] Likewise, to try to teach people to be benevolent and righteous is the same as saying you can

---

[10] Adding a *fei* before *hsing* and translating in accordance with the interpretation of Ch'en Ch'i-yu. But the passage is far from clear.

make them wise and long-lived. A ruler who has proper standards will not listen to such an idea.

You may admire the beauty of a lovely woman like Mao-
ch'iang or Hsi-shih all you like, but it will not improve your
own looks. If you apply rouge, powder, and paint, however,
you may make yourself twice as attractive as you were to begin
with. You may talk about the benevolence and righteousness
of the former kings all you like, but it will not make your
own state any better ordered. But if you make your laws and
regulations clear and your rewards and punishments certain, it
is like applying rouge, powder, and paint to the state.[11] The
enlightened ruler pays close attention to such aids to rule, and
has little time for extolling the ancients. Therefore he does
not talk about benevolence and righteousness.

When the shaman priests pray for someone, they say, "May
you live a thousand autumns and ten thousands years!" But
the "thousand autumns and ten thousand years" are only a
noise dinning on the ear—no one has ever proved that such
prayers add so much as a day to anyone's life. For this reason
people despise the shaman priests. Similarly, when the Confucians of the present time counsel rulers, they do not praise
those measures which will bring order today, but talk only of
the achievements of the men who brought order in the past.
They do not investigate matters of bureaucratic system or law,
or examine the realities of villainy and evil, but spend all their
time telling tales of the distant past and praising the achievements of the former kings. And then they try to make their
words more attractive by saying, "If you listen to our advice,
you may become a dictator or a king!" They are the shaman
priests of the rhetoricians, and no ruler with proper standards

[11] The rhythm of the sentence is awkward and the parallelism faulty; it
is probable that something has dropped out of the text.

will tolerate them. Therefore the enlightened ruler works with facts and discards useless theories. He does not talk about deeds of benevolence and righteousness, and he does not listen to the words of scholars.

Nowadays, those who do not understand how to govern invariably say, "You must win the hearts of the people!" If you could assure good government merely by winning the hearts of the people, then there would be no need for men like Yi Yin and Kuan Chung[12]—you could simply listen to what the people say. The reason you cannot rely upon the wisdom of the people is that they have the minds of little children. If the child's head is not shaved, its sores will spread;[13] and if its boil is not lanced, it will become sicker than ever. But when it is having its head shaved or its boil lanced, someone must hold it while the loving mother performs the operation, and it yells and screams incessantly, for it does not understand that the little pain it suffers now will bring great benefit later.

Now the ruler presses the people to till the land and open up new pastures so as to increase their means of livelihood, and yet they consider him harsh; he draws up a penal code and makes the punishments more severe in order to put a stop to evil, and yet the people consider him stern. He levies taxes in cash and grain in order to fill the coffers and granaries so that there will be food for the starving and funds for the army, and yet the people consider him avaricious. He makes certain that everyone within his borders understands warfare and sees to it that there are no private exemptions[14] from military service; he unites the strength of the state and fights

---

[12] For Yi Yin, see above, p. 94, n. 3; for Kuan Chung, see above, p. 33, n. 4, and p. 94, n. 3.

[13] Emending the *fu* in the text to the *fu* which means "increasingly."

[14] Adding *she* after *chieh* and translating in accordance with the interpretation of Ch'en Ch'i-yu.

fiercely in order to take its enemies captive, and yet the people consider him violent. These four types of undertaking all insure order and safety to the state, and yet the people do not have sense enough to rejoice in them.

The ruler seeks for men of superior understanding and ability precisely because he knows that the wisdom of the people is not sufficient to be of any use. In ancient times Yü opened up channels for the rivers and deepened the waterways, and yet the people gathered tiles and stones to throw at him; Tzu-ch'an opened up the fields and planted mulberry trees, and yet the men of Cheng spoke ill of him.[15] Yü profited the whole world, Tzu-ch'an preserved the state of Cheng, and yet both men suffered slander—it is evident from this, then, that the wisdom of the people is not sufficient to be of use. In appointing men, to seek among the people for those who are worthy and wise; in governing, to try to please the people—methods such as these are the source of confusion. They are of no help in ensuring good government.

[15] Yü, the founder of the Hsia dynasty, was supposed to have fixed the courses of the rivers and rescued China from a great flood. Tzu-ch'an (d. 522 B.C.), chief minister of the state of Cheng, introduced various agricultural reforms which were at first much opposed by the people but which eventually brought benefit to the state.

INDEX

Administration, 5 ff.; *see also* Authority; Laws; Ministers; Power; Punishments; Rewards; Rights; Ruler

Agriculture, 7, 95–116 *passim*

Ai, duke of Lu, 102

Allies, reliance on, as source of peril, 49, 68–70

An, king of Han, 2, 3

An-hsi, king of Wei, 21–22

Artisans, 116–17

Attendants, danger to ruler from, 43, 46

Authority, 102 ff.

Barbarians, Western, 97

Baseness of manner, 49, 52–53

Bedfellows, danger to ruler from, 43, 46

Benevolence, 99 ff.

Book of Documents, 82

Book of Lord Shang, 4, 7–8, 110 *n*

Book of Odes, 82

Cap-and-girdle states, 22

Chang Meng-t'an, 57–60

Chang Yi, 68

Ch'ang-p'ing (city), 123

Change, necessity of, 96–117 *passim*

Chao (state), 2, 21, 56–62 *passim*, 123

Chao, king of Yen, 21

Chao, marquis of Han, 32

Chao Chia, 56–57, 61

Chao-ling (city), 21

Chao Ma-fu, 123

Ch'en Chen, 69

Ch'en Ch'i-yu, 14–15, 25 *n*, 27 *nn*, 42 *n*, 101 *n*, 124 *n*, 126 *n*, 128 *n*

Ch'eng T'ang, 76 *n*

Chi (city), 21

Ch'i (state), 4, 21–22, 65 *n*, 66, 94, 100, 101

Ch'i River, 21

Ch'i-tiao, 119–20

Ch'i-tiao Family School, 118

Chiao-chih (region), 63

Chieh, king of Hsia dynasty, 52, 65, 96

Chien, duke of Ch'i, 31, 65 *n*

Chien, lord of Chao, 57

Chih, Robber, 103

Chih Kuo, 60–62

Chih mode, 54

Chih Po Yao, 56–62

Ch'ih-yu (god), 55

Children, danger to ruler from, 84–86

Chin (state), 6, 53, 55, 94

Chin-yang (city), 57–61

Ch'in (state), 4, 68–70, 114, 123 *n*

Ch'in, king of, *see* First Emperor of the Ch'in

Ch'in dynasty, 11–12

Ching (state), 101

Ching, duke of Ch'i, 65 *n*

Ch'ing Feng of Chi, 52

Cho (city), 21

Chou (state), 5, 94, 114

Chou, king of Yin dynasty, 52, 54, 65, 96

Chou dynasty, rulers of, 88–89

Ch'u (state), 21–22, 69–70

Ch'u Mountains, 80

Ch'ü, horses of, 51–52

Chüan (music master), 53–54

Chuang, king of Ch'u, 21–22

Chüeh mode, 55

Ch'ui-chi, jade of, 51–52

Chung-hang family, 56

Chung-liang Family School, 118

Chung-shan (state), 21

Ch'ung-erh, prince of Chin, 70–72: *see also* Wen, duke of Chin

Confucians, 105, 118–27 *passim*
Confucius, 102, 106, 123
Consorts, danger to ruler from, 84–86
Courtesy, failure in, as source of disaster, 50, 52–53, 70–72
Cranes, black, 54–55
Crow, in the sun, 86 *n*
Deeds (results), 32, 39, 91–93
Dictators, Five, *see Pa,* Five
Doctrines, contradictory, 118 ff.
Drill Man, 96
Dry Valley, 53
Eclipses, 86 *n*
Elders, danger to ruler from, 43–44, 46
Eloquence, 100
Extravagance, 62–65
Fa (laws), 7–8
Fa-chia school, *see* Legalist school
Fan family, 56
Fang-ch'eng (city), 21
Father of the Ruler, *see* Wu-ling, king of Chao
Faults, ten, 49–72
Favor, *see* Rewards
Feng (region), 99
Fire, discovery of, 96
First Emperor of the Ch'in, 2, 3, 11–12, 69, 82 *n*
Five *Pa, see Pa,* Five
Flood, control of, 96
Forms, Han Fei Tzu's concept, 9
Funerals, 119
Gain, petty, 49, 51–52
Goods, abundance and scarcity of, 97–98
Greed, 49, 56–62
Han (state), 1–2, 21, 56–62 *passim,* 68–70
Han, ruler of, 68–70
Han Fei Tzu, life of, 1–3; philosophy of, 4 ff.
Han Fei Tzu, 3, 4, 13–14; characteristics of, 14

Han River, 99
Han Tzu, see Han Fei Tzu
Han Yü, 13
Handles, two, of government, 30–34
Hao (region), 99
Heaven (Tao), 37
History, use of, by philosophers, 11
Ho, Mr., 80–81
Horizontal Alliance, 111–12, 114
Houses, invention of, 96
Hsi-ch'i, 84
Hsi Fu-chi, 70–72
Hsi P'eng, 67–68
Hsi-shih, 127
Hsi Yen, *see* Kuo Yen
Hsia dynasty, 63
Hsiang, king of Yen, 21 *n*
Hsiang, viscount of Chao, 57–62
Hsiang-fu Family School, 118
Hsiang-li Family School, 118
Hsiao, duke of Ch'in, 82–83
Hsien, duke of Chin, 51–52, 70 *n,* 71–72, 84
Hsing-ming (forms and names), 9
Hsü (state), 99
Hsü, ruler of, 52
Hsüan, viscount of Wei, 56–57, 59–61
Hsün Hsi, 51–52
Hsün Tzu, 2, 11, 14
Hu (state), 77
Hua-yang (city), 123
Huai, king of Ch'u, 69
Huan, duke of Ch'i, 5, 21–22, 33, 34, 94, 128 *n*
Huan-hui, king of Han, 2
Hui-wen, king of Chao, 84
Human nature, Legalist view of, 10–11
Infatuation, with women musicians, 49, 62–65
Interest, public and private, conflict between, 104 ff.
Jade, of Mr. Ho, 80–81

Jao Chao, 78
Jung (land), 62–65
Jung (tribe), 52
Jung tribe, king of, 62–65
K'ai-fang, prince of Wei, 67, 68
K'ang, viscount of Han, 56, 59–61
Kao-lang (territory), 57
Kao Yen, *see* Kuo Yen
Kinfolk, danger to ruler from, 43–44, 46
Knights, 105
Kou-chien, king of Yüeh, 33, 86
Ku-yang, 50–51
K'uai, king of Yen, 33, 34
Kuan (state), 21
Kuan Ch'i-ssu, 77–78
Kuan Chung, 4, 5, 66–68, 94, 110, 128
Kuan Lung-feng, 65
Kuan Tzu, 4, 110 *n*
K'uang (music master), 53–55
Kun, minister of Hsia dynasty, 96
Kung, duke of Ts'ao, 70–72
Kung, Honest, 105–6
Kung, king of Ch'u, 50
Kung Chih-ch'i, 51
Kung-chung P'eng, 68–70
Kung-kung (tribe?), 100
Kung-sun Yang, *see* Wei Yang
Kuo (state), 51–52
Kuo Yen, 94
Lao Tzu, 13
Laws, 22–29, 39–40, 90–91, 104–11 *passim*
Learning, Confucian and Mo-ist, 118–29
Legalist school, 4–5, 6 ff.; failure in practice, 12
Li, duke of Chin, 50
Li, king of Ch'u, 80
Li, Lady, 70 *n*, 84
Li Hill, 52
Li Ssu, 2, 3
Li Tui, 84

Liao (secretary), 64
Liao, W. K., 15
Ling, duke of Wei, 53–55, 78–79
Ling, king of Ch'u, 33, 52–53
Literature, technical, 14
Liu T'ao, 13
Logic, school of, 9
Lou-chi, 103
Love, of king for the people, 101–2
Loyalty, petty, 49, 50–51
Loyang (city), 5
Lu (state), 100
Mao-ch'iang, 127
Mencius, quoted, 121 *n*
Meng Family School, 118
Meng Mao, 123
Merchants, 116–17
Mi Tzu-hsia, 78–79
Miao tribes, 99–100
Military service, avoidance of, 117
Ministers: ruler's relation to, 16–20, 22–29, 30–34, 38–42, 43–48, 87–89, 90–95; disregard of, as source of disaster, 49, 66–68; advice to, on the art of persuasion, 73–79, on counseling rulers, 80–83
Mo-ists, 118–27 *passim*
Mo Tzu, 118–19
Mount Hua, 123
Mount T'ai, 55
Mu, duke of Ch'in, 62–65, 71–72, 76 *n*
Music: as source of disaster, 49, 53–56, 62–65; of Master Yen, 53–54
Musicians, women, 64–65
Names, Han Fei Tzu's concept, 9
Names (words), 32, 36, 39, 91–93
Names, school of, *see* Logic, school of
Nan, king of Chou, 114 *n*
Nest Builder, 96
Officials, *see* Ministers

Orators, 116–17; danger to ruler from, 45
Oratory, art of, 73–79
Ou, Smithy, 123
Pa, Five, 5, 94 *n*
Pao Shu-ya, 66–67
People, the, danger to ruler from, 44, 46–47, 87, 88
Persuasion, art of, 73–79
Pi-fang (god), 55
Pi Kan, prince, 65
Pien Ho, *see* Ho, Mr.
P'ing, duke of Chin, 53–56
P'ing-lu (city), 21
Po-li Hsi, 76
Po Lo, 124
Political science, 4–5
Power, 16–20, 22–29, 30–34, 35–42, 87–88, 100 ff., 125; of ministers, danger to ruler from, 45, 47
P'u River, 53, 54
Punishments, 23, 30–34, 38–41 *passim*, 46–47, 104
Pursuits, baleful, danger to ruler from, 44, 46
Rabbit, 97
Rain Master, 55
Realist school, *see* Legalist school
Results (deeds), 32, 39, 91–93
Rewards, 23, 30–34, 38–41 *passim*, 46–48, 103–4
Righteousness, 99 ff.
Rights, to be reserved by ruler, 18–19, 22–28, 30–34, 39–42, 46–48, 87–88
Ruler: ideal, of Confucianism and Mo-ism, 9–10, of Legalism, 10; Way of, 16–20, 22–29, 30–34, 35–42, 90–95, 97–117 *passim*, 119–27 *passim*; dangers to, 18–19, 22–28, 30–34, 38–42, 43–48, 84–89
Sage, as ruler, 16–20, 96–117 *passim*

Sage, Taoist, 10
Scholars, 116–29 *passim*
Shang, Lord, *see* Wei Yang
Shang-chün shu, see *Book of Lord Shang*
Shang (Yin) dynasty, 94
Shang mode, 54
Shang Yang, *see* Wei Yang
Shen (city), 52
Shen Pu-hai, 4
Shen-sheng, 84
Shen Tao, 4
Shih (actor), 84
Shu (principles of government), 8–9
Shu Chan, 70–72
Shu-tiao, 33, 34, 67, 68
Shun (emperor), 63, 96, 99–100, 118–19
Soldier-deserter of Lu, 106
South Gate Palace, 68
Spring and Autumn Annals, 88
Spring and Autumn Annals of T'ao Tso, quoted, 85
Standards, of government, 21–29
States: disordered, customs of, 116–17; neighboring, danger to ruler from, 45–46, 47
Ssu-ma Ch'ien, 2
Sui-yang (city), 21
Sun Family School, 118
Sun Tzu, 110 *n*
Sun Wu, 110
Sung, farmer of, and the rabbit, 97
Sung, rich man of, and his neighbor, 77–78
Sung, ruler of, 31
Sung Jung-tzu (Sung Chien; Sung K'eng), 120
Supernatural events, accompanying music, 54–55
Swordsmen, 117
T'ai-kung, 94
Takeuchi Teruo, 15
Tan-t'ai Tzu-yu, 123

T'ang, king of Yin (Shang) dynasty, 94, 96, 128 n
T'ang-fu (region), 68
Tao, king of Ch'u, 81–83
Tao-te-ching (Lao Tzu), 13
Taoism, 9–10; language of, in *Han Fei Tzu*, 35 n
T'ao (region), 21
T'ao Hung-ch'ing, 40 n
Teng-ling Family School, 118
Thrift, 62–65
Ti (tribe), 52
Tien family, 65 n
T'ien Ch'ang, 31, 34, 65 n, 109
T'ien Ch'eng, viscount of Ch'i, 65–66
Toad, in the moon, 86 n
Travel, danger to ruler from, 49, 65–66
"Treatise on Literature" (*History of the Former Han*), 13
Ts'ai (city), 21
Ts'ai (territory), 57
Ts'ai Yü, 123
Ts'ang Chieh, 106
Tso, crown prince of Sung, 52
Tuan Kuei, 56, 61
Tung Kuan-yü, 57–59
Tzu-ch'an (Tzu-ch'ang), 128
Tzu-chang School, 118
Tzu-chih, 33, 34
Tzu-fan, 50–51
Tzu-han, 31, 109
Tzu-k'uai, *see* K'uai, king of Yen
Tzu-kung, 100
Tzu-ssu School, 118
Uno Tetsuto, 15
Vermin, five, 96–117
Vertical Alliance, 111–13, 114
Villainies, eight, 43–48
Waley, Arthur, 15
Wang Liang (charioteer), 86
Wang Wei, 47 n
Way, the, *see* Ruler: Way of

Wei (state), 2, 21, 22, 56–62 *passim*, 114, 123
Wei Yang (Kung-sun Yang; Lord Shang), 4, 82–83, 94
Wen, duke of Chin, 94; *see also* Ch'ung-erh, prince of Chin
Wen, king of Ching, 99
Wey (state), 114
Wind Earl, 55
Wisdom, 100
Words (names), 32, 39, 91–93
Writing, invention of, 106
Wu, duke of Cheng, 77
Wu, king of Chou, 54, 94, 96
Wu, king of Ch'u, 80
Wu Ch'i, 81–83, 110
Wu-ling, king of Chao, 84
Wu Tzu, 110 n
Yang Chu, 121 n
Yao (emperor), 63, 96, 97, 118–19
Yellow Emperor, 55; quoted, 40
Yellow River, 21
Yen (music master), 54
Yen (state), 21, 22, 114
Yen, king of Hsü, 99, 100
Yen Cho-chü, 65–66
Yen Family School, 118
Yen-ling (region), 50
Yen-ling Sheng, 57
Yi-ya, 33, 34, 67, 68
Yi-yang (city), 68–70
Yi Yin, 76, 94, 128
Yin (state), 94
Yin (Shang) dynasty, 63–64, 94 n
Yin To, 56
Yu-jung, 52
Yu-min, 52
Yu-tu (region), 63
Yu Yü, 62–65
Yü (emperor), 96, 97–98, 99, 129
Yü (state), 51–52
Yü, duke of, 51–52
Yüan, duke of Sung, *see* Tso, crown prince of Sung
Yüeh-cheng Family School, 118